Kill Phil

Kill Phil

The Fast Track to Success in No-Limit Hold 'Em Poker Tournaments

Blair Rodman
and
Lee Nelson

Foreword by Phil Hellmuth, Jr.

Huntington Press
Las Vegas Nevada

Kill Phil

The Fast Track to Success in
No-Limit Hold 'Em Poker Tournaments

Published by
Huntington Press
3665 S. Procyon Ave.
Las Vegas, NV 89103
Phone (702) 252-0655
e-mail: books@huntingtonpress.com

Copyright ©2005, Blair Rodman and Lee Nelson

ISBN: 0-929712-24-2

Cover Photo supplied by Larry Grossman
Cover Logo supplied by Michelle Pelletier of DC Graphics

Cover Design: Bethany Coffey
Interior Design & Production: Laurie Shaw

Dedication

Blair dedicates this book to two who passed on in 2005: my Mom, the English teacher, who would have been proud to see her son in print; and Bobby Hamilton, whose good and gentle soul left us all too soon.

Lee dedicates this book to: my devoted wife, my aspiring son, and my recently departed father and mother.

Acknowledgments

We'd like to thank a number of people who made this book possible. We appreciate the many people in the poker world who've helped develop the game to the point where it is today. Our thanks go to the late Benny Binion, and Jack Binion, for creating and promoting the World Series of Poker, and Doyle Brunson, the "grandfather" of the modern game.

We're grateful to Phil Hellmuth for the Foreword and for allowing us to use his picture on the cover.

We greatly appreciate the players who read our manuscript and have provided recommendations and blurbs for the book.

We'd like to express our appreciation to Peter Wong, Spencer Mohler, and Chris Compton for their input on the manuscript and help in testing the Kill Phil principles in actual play, both live and online, and to Maurie Pears of pokernetwork.com for his help with promotion in Australasia.

Thanks to our friends at Huntington Press for going

the extra mile with this project, notably Deke Castleman, Bethany Coffey, Sasha Baugess, and Laurie Shaw.

And a special appreciation to our friend Anthony Curtis, the hardest-working man in the business, without whom there would be no Kill Phil.

Thanks to Lee's wife, Pen, for typing large portions of the manuscript, and to Pen, along with Blair's wife Roxxie, who put up with us through the ordeal of writing, re-writing, editing, and re-editing *ad nauseum*. Without your love, it would have been hard to persevere through the ordeal of writing a book.

To all of you, and any we may have inadvertently overlooked, thanks ever so much for making this labor of love possible.

Contents

Part One
Beginning Considerations

Part Two
The Kill Phil Beginner Strategies

Part Three
The Kill Phil Intermediate Strategies

Part Four
Advanced Kill Phil Strategies

Foreword
by Phil Hellmuth, Jr.

One of the Phils Fires Back

First of all, let me—Phil Hellmuth, Jr.—say this, "Do not take the title of this book literally! No one wants that fate to befall any of the Phils. Rather, the authors want you to beat us Phils out of our chips at the poker tables."

I admit I was amused, and flattered, when I heard that a book with such a title would soon be circulating through the poker world. "Kill Phil" obviously refers to me to some extent, but with Phil "Unabomber" Laak, Phil Gordon, and especially young phenom Phil Ivey also sharing the name, I wasn't sure what portion of the attribution I could assume.

To be honest, I would prefer that this book had found no publisher. I mean, who wants a credible book out there by tough-as-nails poker players (Blair Rodman and Lee Nelson) telling the world exactly how to beat you? The strategy they present here is simple and effective. It's basically an extension of one of the tactics that David Sklansky presented in his book, *Advanced Texas Hold 'Em Tournament Strategy*.

The tactics are about putting pressure on the great players by moving them all-in before the flop. In this way, you're forcing them to commit all their chips, which is something that none of the great players ever wants to do. Personally, I will go to great lengths to avoid putting all of my chips at risk in any hand, because when I'm all-in, then it's possible for me to be eliminated.

In 2004 I was even exploring the theory of folding hands where I was actually a 4½-1 favorite. For example, I folded pocket queens in the main event of the WSOP (World Series of Poker) even though I thought my opponent had a smaller pair. In that particular case, I was right: My opponent had pocket sevens, giving me a 17% chance to be eliminated. If I'm going that far to avoid being all-in, then it's correct for you to move all-in on me almost every hand. Even when I gave up the tactic of folding a 4½-1 favorite (I have to put the chips in sometime!), I was still going to great lengths to avoid moving all-in.

In many of the tournaments that I've won, I've been all-in—and called—less than three times, and I'm proud of this distinction. Rodman and Nelson understand this and they're teaching you to put me all-in, so that I can fold one more strong hand—and you can win the pot by bluffing me. If enough people read this book, then I'll have to change my tactics, the tactics that have worked so well for so long, and the "Kill Phil" title will have earned real meaning: It will have forced me to change my game!

What was I to do when I was asked to write a foreword or jacket blurb for this book? Ignore its existence? Say no and walk away? After all, it did have my name on it, and what the heck, I'm a promoter! So I chose to read it over and then decide what to do. If it was good, then maybe I would recommend it.

With all kinds of books out there on the subject of poker strategy, I cannot and will not recommend too many of them. (Of course, I recommend the books that I have written!) Too often, a good writer, but mediocre poker player, has written a book that has some good points, but a lot of bad points as well. Rodman and Nelson truly have been through the wars and understand the game. So even though the title of this book is a bit unfriendly to me, I'm recommending that you buy it.

When you've completed your poker education, bring on your best game! I'll be waiting for you at the biggest and most prestigious poker tournaments in the world. Just don't take the title literally!

Good Luck,
Phil Hellmuth, Jr.

INTRODUCTION

*Poker is like sex—everyone thinks they're the best at it,
but only a few actually know what they're doing.*
　　　　　　　—Layne Flack

Poker, baby! No longer does the mention of this game evoke images of smoky back rooms, card sharps, and low-lifes. Nowadays, bring up the subject of poker to nearly anyone and you'll wind up talking about no-limit hold 'em (NLH), the World Poker Tour (WPT), the World Series of Poker (WSOP), or one of the many other televised poker shows. Big-name players of the day have become TV stars. Win a nationally televised tournament and suddenly everyone knows your name. The biggest names, like Gus Hansen, Howard Lederer, Daniel Negreanu, Annie Duke, and of course, the "Phils"—Hellmuth, Ivey, etc.—are living the lives of celebrities. They hang with Hollywood stars, get preferred treatment, sign autographs, and garner lucrative endorsement deals.

No less than Ben Affleck and Tobey Maguire have

won big-time poker tournaments. Affleck pocketed a cool $350,000 for winning a major event in Los Angeles, and Lord knows he needs the money! Almost any day in L.A. you'll find a big-name star in one of the huge card rooms. The star-studded cast playing in the last two World Series in Las Vegas would make a film producer drool: James Woods, Leonardo DiCaprio, Gabe Kaplan, Matt Damon, and, of course, Ben Affleck. In 2005, Jennifer Tilley beat 600 other ladies to win a coveted bracelet and more than $158,000. There's even a TV show dedicated entirely to celebrity poker.

The money involved in poker today is staggering. First prize at the 2004 WSOP main event was $5 million and in 2005 it was a cool $7.5 million. No other sporting event comes close. Winning poker's World Series is worth more than winning Wimbledon, the Masters, and the Kentucky Derby combined! Players from all parts of the globe vie for multiple hundreds of thousands of dollars every *week* in poker tournaments around the world. TV audiences thrive on the excitement, as hidden cameras that reveal the players' cards allow the viewers to get into the game. It's like the ultimate "Survivor" show, as players use every trick in the book to send their competition home. The hundreds of thousands of dollars (sometimes a million or more) in cash dramatically stacked up on the green-felt tables goes to the last man (or woman) left standing—it's a seductive arena. Meanwhile, online tournaments can now attract more than 2,000 players at a time, and they continue to grow. Big money, movie stars, glamorous venues, television—no wonder poker is exploding.

And the phenomenon shows no signs of slowing down. Today, an estimated 50 million Americans play poker. This American pastime has become a worldwide mania, especially when played in the form that's all the rage—no-limit hold 'em. This is the game played in virtually all major tournaments today. Teaching you how to compete in no-limit hold 'em tournaments is the focus of this book. But not *just* compete; you'll also learn how to win! That's right. Assiduously applied, the principles you learn here will give you a real shot at the big money.

Once you've cultivated the necessary skills, the tournaments you see on TV aren't out of reach. There's no special qualifying. You don't have to be drafted or invited. All it takes is the money to enter and the guts to sit down and play. Coming up with the money is your job. Providing you with an approach to playing that will give you a chance, regardless of your level of experience, is ours.

Think about the big-name players you've seen on TV. Do they really have that big an edge over a player who's relatively new to the game? Certainly, they have an advantage in knowledge and experience. But because of the fundamental nature of no-limit tournaments, if you know how to tailor your game to your own level of experience, you can compete in the no-limit arena with a very real chance of success. The application of certain key concepts allows you first to level the playing field, then move to a point where you become a player to be feared—especially by the best players! Imagine walking up to a table and hearing a player you recognize from TV say something like, "Oh, no, not *you*." Wouldn't that be fun? It's possible, because it's the *style* of play that they fear. The style you'll learn from reading this book. We show you the type of player top pros love to see at their table, and the type that they hate. Then we show you how to become the real threat that they detest.

Is it a gimmick, nothing but an over-simplified answer to a complex question? Yes and no. Simple strategies won't give you a long-term edge against the best. But idiosyncrasies in tournament no-limit poker open the door for an inexperienced player who's been properly trained.

We begin with Kill Phil Rookie, a simplified strategy for those who've never played a tournament before. We then move on to Kill Phil Basic. Armed with the basic strategy alone, even a complete novice has a decent shot at getting in the money. Later, we improve on basic by incorporating some powerful poker concepts. Understanding and modifying your game in accordance with these concepts will make you an above average player. Finally, we cover some high-level plays and strategies. Master everything in this book and you could be the next superstar!

Who is *Kill Phil* For?

Kill Phil is for tournament players of all levels.

Complete novices benefit from a strategy that offers a genuine chance of success while they acquire the valuable real-time experience needed to make consistent profits in tournament play. Beginners also benefit from primers on the mechanics of no-limit hold 'em and tournaments in general, as well as the sections on rules and ethics.

Players who've had some experience, but little success, gain from the more advanced strategies, which could put them over the top on their way to success.

"Old-school-style" players who've been struggling learn how to transform their games to the modern style of play.

Players who are competent in the small-ball arena, but are having problems with the nuances of long ball may find the strategies enlightening.

Even already successful players can find valuable nuggets of information.

Regardless of your current level of expertise, the many

pointers throughout this book can help you gain perspective and add ammunition to your playing arsenal.

These pages contain strategies for both online and live play. If you're exclusively an online player, the strategies presented allow you to successfully modify your playing style to adapt to live-tournament play.

Who's Phil?

"Phil" is our code name for any accomplished tournament player. Certainly, several poker superstars are named Phil—Phil Hellmuth, Ivey, Laak, and Gordon among them—but we've lumped all the best players into the Phil category. We had to call them something. Plus, we thought it made for a damn funny title.

Many of the Phils with whom we confided our plans for this book begged us to abort. Their fears were genuine, because this strategy hurts the best players the most. Their lifeblood, the timid inexperienced player, suddenly becomes a threat. That's the essence of Kill Phil—prey becomes predator and vice versa.

Who are We?

Blair Rodman—Blair Rodman has been a full-time professional gambler for more than 20 years and has experienced success in many different areas of the gambling world. He's an accomplished blackjack player, was a member of Stanford Wong's famous gambling-tournament team in the '80s, was part of a highly successful sports-betting group for more than 10 years, and has in-depth knowledge and experience in many other areas of casino advantage play. But his first love is, and always has been, poker—both as a tournament and live-game player. Blair participated in his first WSOP event in 1982. While the pursuit of other gambling interests took him in and out of the poker scene over the years, the recent explosion in the popularity of poker tournaments led him to re-focus his efforts in this area.

Blair has enjoyed a strong reputation for years, having logged several high finishes in major tournaments throughout the country, but it was his 2004 WSOP result that put him on the poker map. In 2004, playing against one of the biggest poker fields in history, Blair had six cashes and made three final tables. He topped it off with a terrific five-day run in the world championship, eventually finishing 54th in the 2,576-player field. Blair continued the pace in 2005, making two final tables on the WSOP circuit, finishing second in a World Poker Tour event at the Reno Hilton, making a Professional Poker Tour final table, and finishing second in the nationally televised Ultimate Poker Challenge from a field made up of many of the world's best players.

Lee Nelson—Lee Nelson is a retired doctor whose medical fields of interest are nutrition and prostate cancer. He's the author of the book *Prostate Cancer Prevention and Cure*. Over the past six years, Lee has performed with remarkable consistently, making final tables with such regularity in international tournaments that he's now known by the nickname "Final Table." At the 2006 Aussie Millions, Lee made three final tables and won the Main Event and it's A$1,295,800 (about $1,000,000us). In 2005 Lee also won two events at the Aussie Millions and won the Party Poker World Open with its $400,000 first prize. Lee has a won a number of other tournaments both live and online, in addition to multiple final-table appearances.

Lee was recognized as the top-ranked player in Australia/New Zealand by PokerNetwork for the period from 2000 to 2005, and is also the leader in 2006. Although playing far fewer events than most touring pros, at the time of this writing Lee ranks 74th in all-time world-wide winnings. Lee has been selected to join 2005 WSOP Champion Joe Hachem on Team PokerStars.

How This Book Came About

Blair Rodman met Lee Nelson through Huntington Press publisher Anthony Curtis. Blair and Anthony have been friends and gambling partners for years, while Lee had authored his prostate-cancer-prevention book for Huntington Press. Anthony knew Lee originally through poker and when Lee decided to author a book on poker tournaments, he came to HP for publishing. What Lee didn't know was that Anthony was already talking to Blair about a poker book (Blair and Lee knew each other by reputation only at this point). Anthony told Lee about Blair's ideas and it was decided that Blair Rodman and Lee Nelson should meet.

It didn't take long for the two authors to come to the conclusion that, together, they could produce a work on tournament poker that would rival anything done by the other professional players. They set to work on the project, putting together a comprehensive outline on no-limit hold 'em poker tournaments.

Time was of the essence, as it was obvious that there would soon be a wave of books on the market. In fact, not long after serious work began, the authors realized that a masterwork on the subject would take far too long to complete, given that the flood of new poker books had already begun. Both concluded that their work, regardless of its merits, would get lost in the shuffle. On the verge of abandoning the project, Blair proposed an alternative—a simple method that would encourage novice players to participate immediately, allowing them to accumulate valuable real-action experience, while maintaining a reasonable chance of success—in essence, a simple, but effective, basic strategy for no-limit hold 'em tournaments.

This approach fit in perfectly with the Huntington Press philosophy. While other gambling-publishing companies often focus on the elite player, over the years HP has catered to the many occasional gamblers that have neither the time nor inclination to become experts, but still want to have a fighting chance. In fairness, the fundamentals of a no-limit tournament basic strategy had been touched on before, most notably by David Sklansky in *Tournament Poker for Advanced Players*. However, the idea hadn't been thoroughly explored.

An outline was prepared and the authors spent several intensive weeks perfecting the strategies. Blair has a long history as a blackjack player; consequently, the Kill Phil basic strategy is similar in many ways to blackjack basic strategy. It takes about as long to assimilate and memorize and is adaptable to strategy cards, which can be used as learning aids or even brought along to the table. Like blackjack, it greatly evens the odds and allows beginners to be competitive, though it doesn't yield a long-term advantage. But just as blackjack basic strategy provides a gateway to that game's powerful count strategies, so too does the Kill Phil basic strategy lead to more powerful and winning strategies for tournament poker.

Finally, our silent partner throughout development of the Kill Phil strategy is a math and gambling expert known in gambling circles as Kim Lee. He worked with us to craft the strategic framework and developed computer programs to generate and test strategies.

More Help

The poker world is changing so rapidly that any book is subject to become outdated quickly. Kill Phil principles are being employed effectively in tournaments by more and more players every day. In order to keep our followers abreast of how these changes relate to the Kill Phil strategy as presented in this book, the authors will maintain a Web site at KillPhilPoker.com, which will provide articles, blogs from our tournaments, a message board, and other interesting features pertaining to the world of poker.

Additionally, as a supplement to this book, condensed versions of the Kill Phil strategies are available on portable strategy cards (see ad, back of book). The cards reference the Rookie, Basic, and Advanced strategies, and can be taken with you to consult or use at the tournament table. There's also an online card for use when playing computer tournaments.

THE ESSENCE OF KILL PHIL

While no-limit hold 'em is a game of infinite complexities, it can be reasonably broken down into two main tactical elements: "small ball" and "long ball."

• Small ballers are singles hitters. They chip away with a variety of intricate strategies. It's a style that requires a great deal of effort and many hours of experience at the tables to reach proficiency. Small ballers are involved in a lot of pots, waiting for the fattest opportunities. If someone presents one, they're poised to go for the kill. The primary province for small ball is *after* the flop.

• Long ball, also known as "big-pot poker," is analogous to home-run hitting. It's an approach that's much easier to learn and implement. It doesn't take years of study and experience to rear back and swing with everything you've got. Long-ball tactics are usually employed *before* the flop.

In NLH cash games, where the blinds are relatively small compared to the average amount of money that can be at stake, small ball is one of the primary weapons of winning players. For example, in a 25-50 no-limit game, most players will have at least $5,000, or more than 66 times the total of the blinds, in front of them. This leads to a lot of post-flop play, as winning just the blinds is essentially insignificant. In tournaments, long ball has a much bigger role, especially late in an event. Early on in tournaments, there's lots of play post-flop, because the blinds at that point are generally small compared to players' stacks. Similar to cash games, this is small-ball time. However, unlike cash games, in order to bring about a conclusion of a tournament in a reasonable amount of time, the blinds increase at set intervals. As a tournament progresses, the blinds (and antes, which are generally instituted fairly early on) become much more significant.

For example, at the start of the second day of the championship event in the 2004 World Series of Poker, the 250-500 blind/100 ante structure meant that if an average stack didn't play a hand, it would be gone in 12 rounds. In this type of situation, the struggle for the pre-flop pot becomes much more important and long ball is a much more viable strategy. By the time the tournament is down to the final table, the blinds and antes are usually so high that all-in moves pre-flop become the norm. It's not uncommon to watch a final table for an hour or more without seeing a single flop.

So, if there are two distinct areas of skill in no-limit hold 'em tournaments and expert players are well-versed in both, which should the aspiring player focus on first?

Let's look.

Small Ball ...

• is complex and difficult to master. The best players have years of the experience necessary to excel in this arena.

• is primarily employed at the earlier levels of a tournament, when pressure from blinds is light and inexperienced players can simply choose not to get involved without a monster hand.

• is not mandatory for success in no-limit hold 'em tournaments.

Long Ball ...

• is formulaic and much easier to learn.

• is the prevalent strategy late in tournaments, when it matters most.

• can be a stand-alone strategy.

• gives the tournament novice the best chance to "get lucky."

The Ball is in Your Court

The answer is clear. No-limit hold 'em tournaments are unique in the poker world, because they offer the novice player a real chance at success—provided he's equipped with the right easy-to-wield weapon. In this book, we provide you with that weapon, along with instructions on how to use it.

Does this mean that small ball is an unnecessary skill? Absolutely not. Small-ball experts are able to use their talents to amass chips at the early levels of a tournament, taken from the less skilled opponents who choose to trade punches with them. The great thing about our method is that it gives you the opportunity to spend hours at the table observing the small-ball experts at work—soaking up knowledge without having to spar with them. Combine this valuable exposure with a study of small ball from some of the excellent poker books now hitting the market and eventually you'll be ready to join the fray. Before you stick your toe in, however, remember that sharks swim in shallow water and it's easy to get bit.

CALLING ALL PLAYERS

Players of differing skill and experience levels will extract value from this book in different ways.

Absolute beginners can build a ground-up strategy starting right here—it's not necessary that you read another poker book first. In fact, you could hold your own in a poker tournament tomorrow, simply by skipping to Chapter 6 and learning the simplified strategy, "Kill Phil Rookie."

If your goal is to become an accomplished player, to get a perspective on the subject, you should begin by reading the introductory topics in Part I, as well as the sections on "Rules" (pg. 211), "Ethics" (pg. 222), and "Basics of No-Limit Texas Hold 'Em" (Appendix II). Then move on to Part II, "The Kill Phil Beginner Strategies," which is the foundation of Kill Phil. With a reasonable amount of study, you should have little trouble becoming proficient in its use.

For online play, we've altered the strategy somewhat to account for the different style you encounter there. The Internet is a wonderful place to hone your game; many of today's young stars began playing online. If that's your preferred arena, practice Kill Phil with its cyber-adjustments in small-buy-in tournaments until you're comfortable with that strategy.

Once you're adept at using the basic strategy, we urge you to move on to the powerful concepts in the "Kill Phil Basic Plus" (Chapter 8). The techniques discussed add much to the Kill Phil strategy's effectiveness, as well as a general understanding of the dynamics of no-limit hold 'em tournaments.

The concepts covered in "Kill Phil Expert" (Chapter 10), combined with an increasing understanding of post-flop play gained through study and observation, puts you well on the road to becoming a successful no-limit hold 'em tournament player. The sample tournament in Chapter 11 helps you to understand how many of the concepts work in real tournament situations.

Sit-n-Go's, or "SNGs," have become very popular, especially on the Internet. They're similar to one-table satellites, which are prominent at major bricks-and-mortar tournaments. For those interested in this variation of tournament, we've included advice on how to tweak the strategy for best results. Several of the players who tested the strategies for us experienced success in this area.

And in a mildly ironic turn, it's our firm belief that one of the prime benefactors of the Kill Phil strategies will be one of the most experienced subsets of the poker universe. Many veteran old-school players are no longer seeing the results they once saw in tournament play. While their small-ball skills are intact, they're failing to adjust to the direction the game has taken. At every tournament these days, more and more players are effectively employing variations of the Kill Phil strategy, and those who don't adjust are being left in the dust.

Blair is a prime example. He was the epitome of the old-school player, having competed in tournaments almost since their inception. While he saw a change taking place in the way tournaments were being played, he couldn't put his finger on it until recently. His change in philosophy coincided with his dramatically improved results beginning in 2004. The exercise of writing this book crystallized these ideas and his success has been ongoing. Players against whom Blair has competed for years now remark on his re-vamped style—though they don't necessarily grasp it. Other old-school players can make similar changes through an understanding of the principles discussed in this book.

Warning: Playing the unaugmented Kill Phil requires an uncommon level of patience. Remember that the strategy is designed to give a new player the best chance of success, a goal best achieved by avoiding unfamiliar (and dangerous) situations. Entering the small-ball fray before you have sufficient experience to sidestep the pitfalls is a recipe for disaster. Accordingly, Kill Phillers must throw away many tempting starting hands in the early going.

It's a difficult thing to do; folding hands as strong as QQ, JJ, or AK in unraised pots pre-flop is bound to frustrate you. Likewise, our advice to make oversized raises with AA and KK will foster comments and puzzled looks from opponents. Some who are frustrated by your style might even make derisive remarks. Even worse, this style of play won't look anything like what you've seen on TV!

Keep three things in mind. First, the TV players are, for the most part, extremely experienced and their games have evolved immensely. Second, what you see on TV is final-table poker, which is vastly different from the early game. And third, the action level on TV is the result of editing to feature big hands. Someone isn't really going all-in with 96 off-suit every hand.

Still, most new players want action and all these things may tempt you to wade into the small-ball arena before you're ready. Don't do it. The time for that will come (we provide a reading list in the Appendix that you can use to learn), but at the outset, don't get too far away from the Kill Phil strategy as written. As a bonus, many of the Kill Phil long-ball strategies will remain the cornerstone of your approach to the game, regardless of your level of advancement.

Another warning: Poker is jargon-intensive. There's a reason for this, as the descriptive nature of the lexicon facilitates an efficient conveyance of ideas. But if you don't know it going in, you'll be lost. Many poker terms are included in this book's extensive Glossary. Some have been given quote marks when they first appear in the text, and a few are accompanied by brief parenthetical explanations. Most, however, simply appear naturally. If you encounter a term that you don't understand, take a moment to consult the Glossary. Doing so enhances your overall understanding of the text, as well as better prepares you for live play.

No doubt many of you will be content with the occasional successes and moments in the sun that Kill Phil can help bring your way. Others will use it as a platform from which to build a world-class game. Whatever your objective, remember to enjoy the challenges, rewards, and entertainment that poker can provide—not to mention the rush of bagging yourself a Phil.

A FINAL WORD

It's absolutely critical that you pay attention to and grasp this seminal point: Kill Phil is not a poker strategy, it's a tournament strategy. If someone reacts to your play by saying, "That's not poker!", simply acknowledge that he's right. There are few true experts in both the cash and tournament arenas. They're related, but separate, skills. There are tournaments in many gambling games—blackjack, craps, baccarat, even keno. The proper strategy in these tournaments is often a distant relative of proper play in a non-tournament setting. Tournaments are a discipline unto themselves. While you may not be as skilled a poker player as your opponents, it's very likely that you'll become a better tournament player—and that's what gets the money.

Part One

Beginning Considerations

1

THE HISTORY OF POKER TOURNAMENTS

Fortune favors the bold.
                —Virgil, *The Aeneid*

Poker tournaments are a relatively new phenomenon in the poker world. While the origins of the game of poker are somewhat sketchy, stretching back centuries, the advent of tournaments can be traced directly to 1969 at the Holiday Hotel in Reno, when between 20 and 30 poker players were invited to the Second Annual Gaming Fraternity Convention. (The First Annual Gaming Fraternity Convention in 1968 was a gathering of casino high rollers who met to compete in a variety of casino games.) There were no structured poker tournaments, just cash play in different games. The event evoked comparisons to the "rendezvous" of the Old West, where denizens of the territories gathered annually to tell tales, play games, and celebrate their free existence. Benny and Jack Binion liked what they saw, envisioning the possibilities of an annual gathering, and when the Holiday was sold in 1970 they acquired the rights to the event. They renamed it the World Series of Poker and moved it to Binion's Horseshoe in Las Vegas.

The early versions of the WSOP were smallish affairs, attended for the most part by a soon-be-extinct breed of road gamblers. They arrived from all around the country, with the majority coming from the Deep South, primarily Texas. Here, too, it wasn't a structured tournament. The men played several different poker games for cash, and at the end, the attendees voted to determine the best player among them. Famous Texas road gambler Johnny Moss was voted #1 in 1970.

In 1971, *L.A. Times* columnist Ted Thackrey and gambler Jimmy "The Greek" Snyder promised the Binions that they could get them nationwide publicity if they staged a formal competition. That year, six players participated in the inaugural World Series of Poker, vying for both the money and the title of "World Champion Poker Player." The game was no-limit Texas hold 'em, which was, not coincidentally, the game of choice of most of the Texas road gamblers. Moss validated the previous year's vote by winning the "freeze-out." The following year eight players entered the final event. This time it was won by Amarillo Slim Preston. Since then, the number of entrants has increased every year but one. In 2005, a whopping 5,619 players anted up $10,000 each for a shot at the money and fame.

Also in 1972, other events began to be added as preliminaries to the no-limit hold 'em final. The book *The Championship Table* by Dana Smith, Tom McEvoy, and Ralph Wheeler chronicles the WSOP from 1970 through 2002. It makes for interesting reading, especially some of the interviews with the early participants (credit for the account of the origins of the WSOP goes to Doyle Brunson's *Super System 2*).

Poker tournaments remained primarily the province of the Horseshoe's WSOP throughout the '70s. As its popularity increased during the '80s, executives of other casinos' poker operations saw the profit potential of staging poker tournaments. The next major event was the "Grand Prix of Poker" at the Golden Nugget, the natural result of Steve Wynn's fascination with the game. Other significant tournaments around that time were the Stardust's "Stairway to the Stars," Amarillo Slim's "Super Bowl of Poker," which began in Lake Tahoe before moving to Caesars Palace in Las Vegas, and Bob Stupak's "America's Cup" tournament at Vegas World.

The first time a WSOP final table was videotaped was in 1973, and in later years it was televised on ABC's "Wide World of Sports" and ESPN. Over the years, televised poker tournaments enjoyed a steady increase in popularity, but never really caught the fancy of the general public. For the casually interested, it was about as exciting as watching checkers on TV.

The inflection point for poker, of course, was the hole-card camera. Knowing the players' hole cards while watching them make crucial decisions turned poker into high drama. The idea had been kicked around for years and had been put into use on the show "Late Night Poker" in the U.K., as well as a few other events, such as the "World Heads-Up Poker Championship" in Vienna in June 2001. For the most part, however, players objected to the idea of letting people see their cards (and, thus, get a line on their play). Then, successful businessman and long-time high-stakes gambler Lyle Berman was approached by TV producer Steve Lipscomb with an idea for a high-quality televised poker show employing the hole-card camera. Players who didn't agree to let their hole cards be shown would be excluded from the tournaments. Most players finally saw the potential and agreed to the format. The first World Poker Tour event was held in late May 2002 at Bellagio in Las Vegas. The game, of course, was no-limit hold 'em. Berman and Lipscomb packaged a classy high-production-value poker show and they made their big breakthrough when they sold the package to cable TV's Travel Channel. With the TV debut of the WPT on a Sunday night in March 2003, poker changed forever.

The World Poker Tour Effect

The scenario: Millions of viewers each week watch the six fortunate players who've maneuvered their way through a large field of participants to sit at the final table of a WPT event. They watch as players make moves to steal the blinds and antes with weak hands, move all-in with all kinds of hands, and often make huge bluffs with nothing. The fact that the TV audience is privy to the players' hole cards while they posture, stare down opponents, and talk trash results in tension-filled theater. When the inevitable showdown occurs, the involved players, as well as the nationwide audience, hold their collective breath until the winner is determined. The action continues along these lines until one player has all the chips.

One of the hallmarks of the WPT is its emphasis on creating personalities. Successful players become stars. Multiple winner Gus Hansen was voted one of *People* magazine's 50 sexiest personalities in 2004. The names Negreanu, Ivey, and Hellmuth are on the tip of every poker aficionado's tongue.

The phenomenal success of the WPT has led to an explosion in the popularity of poker. The weekly WPT telecasts quickly became the Travel Channel's highest rated show. Other TV networks saw the potential and followed suit. ESPN amped up its coverage of the World Series of Poker. Fox got in on the act with tournaments staged for TV. NBC even used a poker show as a lead-in to the Super Bowl! Poker fans can watch televised poker nearly every day and young people are taking to the game in droves. The millions of casual poker players who, in the pre-WPT era, might have gotten together once a month and played small stakes for some laughs are now taking the game seriously. Poker has gone mainstream.

However, TV gives a skewed view of the game. What many of the uninitiated don't understand when watching televised poker is that there are different stages in no-limit hold 'em tournaments. In most broadcasts, viewers see only the final stage, which is the final (championship) table. Play in early stages of tournaments is, and should be, far different from final-table play. Here's why.

The opening blind structure of a tournament in which each player starts with 10,000 is usually 25-50. This means you have to put up only .75% of your stack in blinds each round. In the middle stages—let's use the WSOP for an example—if the average stack is 25,000 and the blinds are 400-800 with a 100 ante, a player with an average stack must put up about 10% of his stack each round! At the final table, there'll generally be one or more players short on chips who must put up 25%, or more, of their stacks each round. Plus, at a table that's less than full, the situation is exacerbated as the blinds come around more often. This leads to the aggressive and seemingly desperate plays seen by millions of poker fans. While it makes for compelling television, viewers are rarely exposed to the more complex and less aggressive style of play traditionally employed at earlier stages of tournaments, when pressure from the blinds and antes is less pronounced. These days, many new players base their approach to the game on the televised poker they've seen.

As these newbies have gravitated to playing in online and real-money no-limit tournaments, their TV-generated perceptions and resulting style of play have affected the way no-limit hold 'em tournaments are played. Old-style players who fail to understand and adjust to the new style of play risk getting left in the dust.

2

UNDERSTANDING NO-LIMIT HOLD 'EM

Hold 'em is to stud what chess is to checkers.
—Johnny Moss

Doyle Brunson describes no-limit hold 'em (NLH) as "the Cadillac of poker games." This is undoubtedly the case in cash games, where the blinds may be as little as 1%, or less, of each player's average chips. This structure gives rise to myriad complex plays, strategies, traps, and bluffs, and quickly separates the experts from the wannabes (and the wannabes from their bankrolls).

Whether the Cadillac comparison applies to no-limit hold 'em tournaments is a more debatable issue. There are varying opinions among poker pros. Some favor no-limit, while many experts feel that in a tournament, pot-limit hold 'em requires more skill. Still others contend that a mixed-game/limit format like HOSE (hold 'em, Omaha hi-lo, stud, and stud-8 or better), where the games rotate every thirty minutes or so, is the greatest test of tournament skill.

In the early stages of a no-limit hold 'em tournament, play greatly resembles what you would find in most no-limit cash games. However, the necessity of whittling the field down to one eventual winner puts constant pressure on players to gamble for the escalating blinds and antes, more so than most experts would like. Competing for these chips is an essential part of winning. Once an NLH tournament progresses to this point, the bone that sticks in the pro's throat is the pre-flop all-in bet. Experts want to win as many chips as possible without putting too much at risk—unless, of course, they have the best of it. Amateurs are best served by moving all-in, which puts their more experienced foes to a guess and exposes them to a potentially fatal risk. Being on the receiving end of this ploy dramatically limits a pro's maneuverability. It's either call or fold—that's it! All the fancy plays in a top expert's arsenal are reduced to a simple in-or-out decision, and it's often for a big percentage (perhaps all) of his chips. Good players hate being put into this situation.

Experts can ruminate all they want about the relative skill factor of NLH, but the dominance of no-limit hold 'em in television coverage and online play has firmly established it as *the* game—period! They've got no choice. No-limit is where the money is; it also holds out the rewards of celebrity status and book and even movie deals. These considerations reduce skill-factor arguments to the realm of academic musings.

Not surprisingly, what many pros view as the "flaw" in no-limit tournament poker, the ability to make an all-in bet at any time, is what can catapult an inexperienced player from obscurity to the final table. Let's examine how this tactic can negatively impact the high expected value (expected return on their money) that tournament specialists normally enjoy.

BULLYING THE BIG BOYS

It's been estimated that the highest echelon of no-limit hold 'em tournament players can expect a four-fold, or higher, average return on their entry fees (see *Harrington on Hold 'Em* by Dan Harrington and Bill Robertie). Experts garner these returns by using their superior skills to amass a large stack of chips, which they use to bully less experienced opponents. The best players are very good at putting pressure on their opponents without jeopardizing their own survival. They rarely risk all their chips without having much the best of it.

Confronting them with all-in bets throws a monkey wrench into their game plan. Their reluctance to gamble with all of their chips without a big edge allows *you* to bully *them*.

Early in tournaments, an expert is particularly unwilling to risk his entire stack in an all-in confrontation unless he clearly has a big advantage. There's too much "dead money" around for him to pick up. As the tournament progresses, this situation may change. As the expert's stack size increases, he can take on smaller stacks without risking all his chips, so he no longer has to be a prodigious favorite. Also, when the blinds and antes are high, he may be forced into "races," because there may not be enough time to wait for more favorable situations. At some point, he has to take a stand and confront aggressive move-in specialists, such as Kill Phil players.

How big a favorite must he be to risk all his chips? Paul Phillips says that he'll never knowingly fold when faced with a bet that puts him all-in if he's at least a 3-2 favorite. Paul has one of the most astute minds in the poker world, so his threshold is probably accurate, but we can test his statement by looking at an example.

In a tournament with 128 entrants, a typical player must double up seven times to win (or the additive equivalent in smaller confrontations). So, if he's even money in each, his chance of success is .5 to the 7th power, or .5 x .5 x .5 x .5 x .5 x .5 x .5 = .0078125. Let's assume a player has a 60% (3-2) chance in all confrontations. Now he's facing .6 to the 7th power, or .0279936; his chances are roughly 3.58 times better. So if a player has 3-4 times the average expected value, he would probably consider a 60% all-in confrontation, but not much less, which confirms Paul's statement. It follows, therefore, that any time a Phil has less than 3-2 the best of it when all his money's at risk, he's getting less than his expected value—i.e., he's taking the worst of it.

In all-in heads-up match-ups, hands that are 3-2 or better include pair-over-pair, such as 77 vs. 44 (more than a 4-1 favorite); hands that "dominate" another, such as AK vs. AQ (about 3-1); and pairs against hands that have a single overcard, such as KK versus AQ (about 9-4). (We're grateful to twodimes.net, an excellent free online site that provides calculations of hand match-ups for a variety of poker games. Throughout the text, we use pot equity when evaluating match-ups, rather than win percentage, because it more accurately takes the effect of tie hands into account.)

Herein lies the rub in NLH. With few exceptions, it's difficult for a Phil to be sure that he's on the right side of one of the above match-ups, so he'll generally avoid all-in situations until he's built up his stack. He'd much rather employ typical small-ball tactics—like picking up pots when no one has a hand or taking flops cheaply and flopping a well-concealed powerhouse—than risk his stack in all-in pre-flop confrontations.

If only a small percentage of the pro's chips are at risk,

being only a small favorite is okay. This frequently arises late in a tournament, when an expert with a big stack takes on a small stack facing elimination. Situations like this can't seriously hurt his stack, so he's willing to get involved with far less than 3-2 the best of it. But when the lion's share of his chips are at stake, many pros will avoid the situation, even when they think they probably have the best hand, unless they're short-stacked and forced to gamble. They reason, simply, that there are better spots for their money. This is why players such as Phil Hellmuth might lay down pocket queens early in a tournament when faced with an all-in re-raise. If his opponent happens to have AK, as is often the case with an all-in re-raise, Phil will be risking all his chips when only a 13-10 favorite. Not big enough. What if the re-raise represents pocket aces or kings? Forget about it! In this case, Phil would be a huge underdog against a player he's never even heard of. No thank you. Not Phil Hellmuth. Not on national TV. Better to muck those queens and wait for a spot when he has the nuts to trap this pretender for all his money. Makes sense. But we're going to show you how to foil his, and every other Phil's, plans.

The Tournament Transition

In the early years of poker tournaments, the fields consisted primarily of the road gamblers. These guys were definitely old school. They didn't come in with highly developed tournament strategies. Rather, they carried their cash-game skills into the tournament arena. As tournaments gained in number and popularity, some players who felt they were better suited to tournament play decided to curtail their side-game action to focus on tournaments alone. The professional tournament player was born.

Today, many new players are learning to play poker in tournaments, developing their style directly from tournament play. Tournament players are coming from all walks of life—high schools, colleges, fraternities, and social groups of all varieties. Tournaments on the Internet are a fertile breeding ground for new players to get in on the action at almost any buy-in level they choose. Many of these players have no idea how the tournament strategies they employ would work in ring games, and unless they have plans to spill over into side-game play, they shouldn't care.

OLD SCHOOL

Players from the old school play tight, solid, selectively aggressive poker. They patiently wait for a hand, then push it for all it's worth. They're not involved in many pots, especially early in a tournament. When they are, they generally have a quality hand. They tend to avoid ambiguous situations, and try to define their opponents' holdings by raising pre-flop in an attempt to eliminate speculative hands, like small pairs and suited connectors. When faced with the pressure of an all-in bet that could knock them out of a tournament, they usually pass unless they've got the nuts or close to it. They steal blinds when they get to amounts that are worth stealing, but usually do so with some kind of hand, like two cards 10 or above or a small pair. Patience, combined with selective aggressiveness and pot-size manipulation, is the backbone of their game.

Old-school players often survive the first day of a major tournament, but rarely amass a big stack. It would be very rare for an old-school player to be leading the WSOP after the first day. Even the great Doyle Brunson in *Super System 2* advocates tight play at early limits. He wants to survive with his bankroll intact, avoiding coin-flip situations for all his chips. He describes a hand in which Phil Hellmuth laid down K♦J♦ on a flop of Q♦-T♦-2♣ rather than call an all-in bet. He agrees with Phil's laydown: Even if he was a favorite in the hand, he feels it's incorrect for a player with Phil's talent to risk all his chips at this stage of a tournament without the nuts. Old schoolers tend to become more aggressive as the blinds and antes increase.

Examples of great old-school players include T.J. Cloutier, Howard Lederer, Dewey Tomko, Russ Hamilton, and Dan Harrington, whose recently released book, *Harrington on Hold 'Em* (Volume I), is a primer on old-school play.

Old-school players thrive on making bets that offer their opponents incorrect pot-odds, which renders calling a bad decision. They also frequently make value bets when they think they have the best hand, but try to leave themselves a way to escape from a hand should they encounter unexpected pressure. Using math, solid play, and randomized calculated bluffs, their modus operandi is to extract maximum value from each hand.

NEW SCHOOL

The new breed subscribes to a different philosophy and it's been paying off. Players like Daniel Negreanu, Gus Hansen, Layne Flack, Phil Ivey, and Ted Forrest typify these new young champions. They're liable to have any hand, in any position, at any time. The high percentage of pots they get involved in is unfathomable to the old-school guys. Defying the T.J. Cloutier motto, "Early in a tournament, tight is right," these guys start mixing it up right from the starting bell. David Sklansky has put forth the theory that the leader after the first day of the championship event at the WSOP has little chance to win, because it tends to be a bad player who's played too many hands and simply gotten lucky. Good new-breed players scoff at this and accept the risks necessary to acquire a big stack early. If they're successful, they then use it to pound on their opponents. They readily embrace the possibility of going wire to wire in any tournament. It seems like they're in nearly every hand and it's virtually impossible to put them on a hand. Let's examine in detail some of the characteristics of new-school players.

Lack of fear of busting out—One of the primary characteristics of new-school players is that they enter tournaments with the idea that their whole stack is in play at all times, readily accepting that they could bust out early. This allows them to make many of the highly aggressive plays that they employ. They maintain this fearlessness throughout the tournament. A player reaching a final table with a huge chip lead is often a new-schooler.

Relaxed hand selection—New-school players get involved in a lot of hands. Their starting-hand requirements are much looser than old-school players. At tournament tables these days, especially in the early stages, you often see two or even three players who seem to be constantly involved in pots, while other players are pretty much on the sidelines waiting for quality hands.

Aggressive tactics—New-school players play their hands very aggressively. Intimidation, bullying, and bluffing are major weapons in their arsenal.

Aggressive play on later streets—Traditionally, in hold 'em, a crucial decision is whether to continue to play after seeing the flop. Players who don't get a good flop generally fold to a bet. Many of the better new-school players, especially if they have good betting position, don't give up so easily. They sometimes call a reasonable bet on the flop with a hand that doesn't appear to merit a call. It's hard to get rid of these guys on the flop. If the turn brings a miracle card, they could win a big pot. If their opponent checks the turn, they can often pick up the pot with a bluff or take a free card if they have a draw.

Play situations rather than cards—They balk at the idea that tournaments should be card-catching contests. Their tactics would often work even if they hadn't looked at their cards!

The following are examples of new-school thinking and tactics.

Raise With a Lot of Hands, Then Bet the Flop; Create Positive Return

Not only do these young guns raise pre-flop with many hands, they also bet most flops. They know that if you're holding two unpaired cards, you're more than a 2-1 underdog to flop either card. If you have a pair and overcards come on the flop, they're aware that you can't stand much heat. They have a full arsenal of plays to put pressure on you. (And on those occasions when you do hit your hand, they might make a concealed monster and bust you.)

> **Key Point**: If you hold two unpaired cards, 68% of the time you won't pair either card on the flop.

For example, if you've played a medium pair and over-cards come on the flop (which is usually the case), a bet on the flop is often enough to get you off the hand. A pair of 8s shrinks right up against K-T-4 when you're faced with a pot-sized bet. Here, their bet on the flop wins the pot.

Gus Hansen, formerly a champion backgammon player, thinks in terms of return on investment. If there's a 68% chance that you'll fold if he bets the flop, he's getting 2.3-1 odds that you'll fold. Since he's betting an amount equal to or less than the size of the pot, he's got a positive return if you fold more than half the time. If you fold more than two-thirds of the time, as you most likely will, he's getting a huge positive return on his investment. Often, he makes bets of only 50%-75% of the size of the pot, increasing his return further still. He probes until he works out the minimum amount required post-flop to pick up the pot, maximizing his return. This amount varies, depending on the table composition.

Players like Gus, Ted, and Daniel come out firing, constantly putting their foes to a decision. Because it's next to impossible to work out what cards these guys are playing, many players simply avoid them unless they've got a monster. Playing this way, if they don't bust out early, new schoolers often accumulate a mound of chips. This allows them the flexibility to call standard-size raises with speculative hands without putting more than 5%-7% of their stack at risk. A few good flops and their mound becomes a mountain. Often, there's no reason to alter their game plan throughout an entire tournament.

Fire a Second Barrel

Because these great new-school players usually bring it in with a raise, they could easily have a hand like a "big ace." So if an ace or a king flops and they bet (as they surely will), you might be up against a really strong hand. Let's say you've got pocket 9s and the flop comes A-4-2. They lead at the pot as usual, but this time you have position and decide to call and see what they'll do on the turn. Many players slow down if they've missed the flop, but not these guys. If they observe any indication of weakness on your part—they're really good at spotting a slight hesitation or other signs of indecision—they fire again on the turn. They do this if they have a hand like AK, giving them top pair and top kicker, or if they have absolutely nothing. If you were in doubt about your 9s before, this additional bet is usually enough to convince you to fold. Now they add even more chips to their stack.

Bluffing twice at a pot is referred to as "firing a second barrel." Many players have the courage to bluff at a pot once, but few have the gumption to fire that second barrel. These guys know that when they bet again on the turn, you've got to respect that second bet as representing a real hand. Quite often they get the desired result: You give up.

And guess what? Even if you muster enough courage to call that second salvo, there's still a third barrel leveled right between your eyes on the river.

Besides representing top pair, there are times when the flop hits their hand in ways that you couldn't possibly suspect. In the above example, when the flop was A-2-4, they could have a hand such as 53 suited. Or on a flop like J-7-3, they could be playing a hand such as 73 suited. You just never know where you're at against these guys and they never seem to slow down and stop betting.

Use Position and the Bluff-Call

Although both old- and new-school players understand the value of position, the new breed uses position in more novel ways. Knowing how aggressive these new stars tend to be, you're reluctant to check the flop to them, unless you've flopped a big hand and are trapping. You know that if you check, these guys will bet and take the pot. So you might decide to take a stab at that pot even though you've missed the flop, just as your aggressive adversaries would.

After all, even though the new-school players could have anything, the flop didn't have to hit their hand—the same 68% chance of not improving on the flop also applies to *them*. So you bet, turning the tables on them, trying to get them to fold. Here's the rub. They often call whether or not they've got any part of the flop just to see what you do on the turn. They might have second or third pair or they might have absolutely nothing. But since you have to act first again on the turn, they call. If you have a real hand (or have the courage to fire a second barrel), they fold if the turn card doesn't help them. But if you check the turn, they pounce like a hungry leopard and snatch that pot away from you. In other words, they may call your bet on the flop with one purpose in mind—to bluff on the turn if you check.

Notice that when they make this play, they have position. You have to act first. They study you. You act, then they react. It can be an intimidating experience, because they might have garbage or the World's Fair. But against these great players, you almost never know. They play both the same way. This creates a major problem for their opponents, even top old-school pros.

Let's look at an example. You have A♠K♣ in early position, bring it in with a raise, and get called by Layne Flack on the button. The flop comes T♦-6♠-4♣. You make a pot-sized bet and Layne calls. Just as you're about ready to abandon ship, the turn card is a miracle ace. You bet, and now Layne moves in for all your money! Now what do you do? He could easily have a hand like aces and sixes, a lower two pair, or a set. He knows that you raised up front and that the ace that came on the turn likely helped you, yet he still moved in. He's put you to the test and if you guess wrong, you're out. This is different from just calling on the flop to bluff on the turn. While he may indeed be bluffing with just a straight draw, he could also have you in very bad shape. In the words of Howard Lederer, "If you play a big pot with Layne, you'd better have a big hand." Is it really worth the risk?

How would a seasoned pro handle a similar situation? At the WPT Championship Event in 2003, with the blinds $100-$200, Doyle Brunson made it $700 to go from the button. Howard Lederer, holding AQ in the small blind, raised an additional $2,000. Doyle called. The flop was Q♠-8♥-6♥. Howard, now with top pair and top kicker, bet $4,000 and Doyle moved all-in. Howard folded! Doyle could have had aces, kings, a set, two pair, a flush draw, or a straight draw. In Howard's mind, it wasn't worth risking all his chips to find out. Even if Doyle had only a flush draw, Howard would lose 35% of the time and be out of the tournament. Against Doyle's stronger possibilities, Howard was a big dog, so he passed. It just wasn't worth the risk (this anecdote was taken from Howard Lederer's Web site: howardlederer.com).

You may be surprised that we use Doyle to exemplify new-school play. Actually, we consider Doyle to be the originator of this type of thinking. He's a strong advocate of constantly pounding away and forcing other players to make a tough decision. Highly regarded new-school players, such as Daniel Negreanu, have credited Doyle's

Super/System as being a pivotal part of their development as poker players.

Have a High Tolerance for Ambiguity

One of the characteristics of new-school players is a high tolerance for ambiguity. Old-school players make plays to define their hands and find out where they're at relative to their opponents. For example, they raise to limit the field and to induce lesser hands, like small pairs and suited connectors, to fold. New-school players make unorthodox plays and take more risks in an attempt to keep their opponents guessing. They often smooth-call a raise with aces or kings pre-flop, disguising the strength of their hand. As we've seen, they may on occasion get hoisted with their own petard, but they're willing to take this risk in order to mask the strength of their hand.

In a small blind-big blind confrontation, they may smooth-call a raise from the small blind with a hand such as AK. If they hit the flop, their opponent may commit a lot of chips before realizing he's beaten. Or they may limp in first position with AK, running the risk of multiple limpers. But if the pot is raised, they may then move in. Since this is the way most players play aces or kings, they usually win a nice pot uncontested. It's very hard to call this bet with less than pocket aces or kings, the very hands that they're representing.

Rely on Ability to Read Players

Complementing their high tolerance for ambiguity, new-school adepts have great ability in reading other players. Sometimes they have a tell on a certain player (see "How to Avoid Tells," pg. 92), but often their read is based on a combination of the betting sequence, the board, and what they know about their opponents' tendencies. Because they're able to assimilate these factors quickly, they form a conclusion about where they stand in a hand. They're confident enough in their ability to read other players that they rely on their reads for making big decisions. They're usually right on target.

Without this skill, new schoolers would be much less able to tolerate the ambiguity involved in not defining their hands. Whereas old-school players use bets and raises to define their opponents' hands, new-school players rely more on their reads. And while their insights into other players' actions are usually accurate, their adversaries have immense difficulties in putting *them* on a hand. This results in a myriad of profitable opportunities for the new generation of poker pros.

Be Creative

New-school players are creative. They mix up their play. Sometimes they make a small bet; sometimes they overbet the pot. The object is to create confusion in the minds of their opponents. You say to yourself, "Why did he make such a small bet? Is it because he's weak and trying to keep the size of the pot down, as he might if he's on a draw, or because he's strong and trying to goad you into raising? It could be either." Constantly mixing up the way he plays, the new-school expert keeps you guessing this way. You're perpetually off balance, wondering if you have the best hand, even when your cards seem strong. Guesswork leads to insecurity and insecurity breeds fear. This is exactly the emotional sequence that these pros are trying to provoke. Once they've got you scared, they're well on their way to absconding with your chips.

Often their betting strategy involves multi-level thinking. They may try to keep the pot small with speculative (drawing) hands, but if contested, are prepared to represent strength in an attempt to blow you off your hand. If they get called, they still have outs.

Say a new-school player brings it in for his usual raise and you decide to call on the button with KQ suited. The flop comes Q♣-5♥-4♥ and he bets half the pot, a weak bet. You've got top pair with a king kicker. You don't know if he's got an overpair, AQ, a set, a draw, or absolute garbage. You decide to make a decent-sized raise to find out where you stand and he immediately moves all-in. In this case his actual hand was 6♠7♠. He would have been happy if you just called his weak bet, allowing him to draw at his straight cheaply, but when you foiled his A plan by raising, he went to plan B—all-in!

Your raise was designed to establish where you stood in the hand and his all-in re-raise was crafted to instill maximum fear in you and to convince you that you're holding a losing hand. This wasn't his preferred way to play the hand, but it sure is a powerful contingency plan when you decide to get feisty. Usually it works and you fold. But even when you don't, he'll still win the pot 34% of the time.

As you can see, he's got a play to counteract your play, keep control of the hand, and, once again, put you to a tough decision for all your chips. As the fear mounts, that KQ can lose its allure and you may find yourself whimpering, "Take it."

As you can see, talented young Turks present so many problems that even expert old-school players find it daunting to play against them. However, we'll soon show you a strategy that neutralizes many of the advantages these players enjoy.

3

THE BENEFITS OF BIG-POT POKER

… the main thing about tournaments is to try to win small pots early, then hope to catch a break or two.
—Stu Ungar, quoted in *The Biggest Game in Town* by Al Alvarez

SMALL BALL

Most good tournament players believe that the ideal strategy is only to play a big pot when having much the best of it. As we've seen, the strategy of keeping pots small until a player has the nuts, or close to it, is known as small ball. Small-ball tactics work best when blinds are small compared to stack size (if the cost of the blinds, or blinds plus antes, per round is less than 10% of the average player's stack, it's small-ball time). In the latter stages of a tournament when blinds and antes become a significant portion of players' stacks, small ball becomes a less significant factor. While small ball is a general concept, it means different things to different types of players.

Old-school players employ small ball as a method of extracting chips through pot-size manipulation. They use opening bets and raises to narrow the possible range of hands their opponents could have. Then, based on those determinations, they proceed accordingly. Their goal is to build their stack gradually through repeated small bets at favorable odds. At the earliest limits, their main chance to get a big stack is through trapping an opponent in a big pot when they have the nuts. For the most part, however, they view the early limits of a tournament as something to get through with their bankrolls intact. Small ball is a means to increase their chances of survival.

For example, a key point in a hand often comes on the turn. Here, the nature of the action can determine whether a pot becomes large or stays relatively small. Say player A raised in late position pre-flop with A♣K♦. The blinds are 50-100 and he makes it 300 to go. He gets called by the big blind (BB). Both players have about 10,000. The flop is K♥-8♣-5♣. The BB checks and player A bets 400. The BB calls. The pot now contains 1,400. The turn brings a 9♣. The BB checks again. If player A bets at this point, he could win the pot right here. He bets 1,200. However, the BB calls the 1,200 and raises 3,200. Now player A has a big decision to make. He has top pair and the nut flush draw, but the BB could easily have a hand that has him beat. Or he could be trying to steal the pot. And if he doesn't improve, player A is facing the prospect of another decision, perhaps for all his chips, on the river. Had he checked the turn, as many old schoolers would in this situation, his chances of losing a big pot are greatly diminished. His risks in giving a free card, or perhaps gaining the amount of a called bet on the turn, are overshadowed by the reduction in overall risk.

New-school players have a different take on small ball. On his Web site, Barry Greenstein credits Phil Hellmuth with pioneering new-school tactics. Barry defines it as "a method of playing a lot of hands and making small bets and raises that keep opponents in the pot, the theory being that [he] will make better decisions than they do on subsequent streets."

The early levels of a tournament are when new-school small-ball experts shine. With small blinds compared to average stack sizes, they have plenty of leeway to mess around in pots without having to commit a large percentage of their chips, as opposed to later in the event, when flops become rare and all-in pots are the norm. Daniel Negreanu, on his Web site fullcontactpoker.com, expressed his consternation at the structure of a major tournament in Atlantic City, which, in an apparent effort to speed up play, had eliminated "the all-important 25-50 limit" at the start of the tournament. Daniel, and other small-ball specialists, such as Hellmuth, Alan Goehring, and Gus Hansen, salivate at the prospect of playing pots with speculative hands that can develop into monsters. They call reasonable raises looking to bust someone who overplays a big pair. They also outplay opponents, often winning pots in which no one has a strong hand. A great player at a table full of tight and timid novices is like a shark in a goldfish pond.

LONG BALL

For the tournament neophyte, big-pot poker is the great equalizer. To understand this concept more fully, it may be helpful to first view play from the standpoint of a tournament virtuoso, Daniel Negreanu. In one of his articles, he makes the following poignant point.

"The right play depends on many variables, one of which is your opponent's skill level. The less skillful your opponent is, the fewer silly risks you should take. Conversely, the stronger your opponent, the more likely you'll be forced to guess and take some calculated risks. It's not easy to nickel-and-dime a great player."

In the same article, Daniel also says, "Let's say I was up against two weak-tight opponents. Playing a big pot in that situation would be silly. I could probably nickel-and-dime or grind out two weak players."

This sums up the thought process of tournament experts. Don't take big risks; grind it out; avoid guesswork—play small ball. They're good at it. No, they're great at it! As Daniel says, his objective is to nickel-and-dime you—to grind you out. To have any chance, you must deny him, and others of his ilk, the opportunity to milk you dry. You accomplish this by forcing them either to play big pots when they don't want to or to throw their hands away. Put in Daniel's own facetious words, "Call me crazy, but I like to see more than just two cards before all my money goes into a pot!" Sorry, Daniel.

When does an expert want to play a big pot? John Juanda clarifies this issue on his Web site. "One of the cardinal rules of big-pot poker [is] don't play a big pot unless you have a big hand. And in case you aren't sure, top pair doesn't even resemble a big hand."

This is consistent with Daniel's stance. Put them together and you have the philosophy of most pros: Nickel-and-dime them, grind them out, and play a big pot only when you have a big hand. It's a consistent winning formula for great players.

But what happens when these guys are faced with a one-trick pony who forces them to either play big pots without the nuts or give up the pot? This throws a monkey wrench into their game plan. By using our formula to play your game, you'll force the pros out of theirs.

> **Key Point**: Good players want to keep most pots small and allow their superior talent to work over the long run, while weaker players should force big pots and big decisions.

Coin Flips

Most no-limit confrontations are heads-up. In a heads-up zero-sum game, your opponent's loss is your gain. In other words, opponents' mistakes cost them money and make you money. Any time a pro plays a pot for all his chips where his expectation is less than his expected return in the tournament from that point on, he's taking the worst of it. Conversely, any time you play a pot for all your chips where your expectation is greater than your overall expectation from that point on, you're getting the best of it. If you're a big underdog overall and you can get even money, or close to it, on a big pot, you're getting a huge overlay. By moving all-in when you decide to play, you force the better players to either *gamble with you* or relinquish any claim to the pot. Moreover, in all but exceptional circumstances, you're putting them to an uncomfortable guess. And if they guess wrong, it may cost them dearly. You may be surprised at how often they decline your gambit and back down.

You don't need to be better than a Phil. You just need to be more dangerous and less easy to consume than his other victims. An old story illustrates this point. Two poker players were out on safari and unarmed when they noticed a lion stalking them. One changed from hiking boots to sneakers. The other incredulously exclaimed, "You don't think you can outrun that lion, do you?" The other replied, "I don't have to outrun him; I just have to outrun you!"

The good small-ball players' goal of using time to allow their edge to manifest is the reason that they prefer slow structures with a lot of time at each level. Just like a casino, the more trials (hands) they have for their edge to become clear, the better they like it. Multiple small trials decrease volatility. Late in a tournament when the blinds and antes are high, small-ball players are more willing to gamble. At the final table, they're often involved (on either side) in a pair-versus-two-overcards all-in confrontation, but not early on. You, as a KP player, don't mind. Your objective is to increase volatility. Against better players, getting in on either side of a pair-versus-two-overcards match-up is the objective, and it increases your expectation of making the money while decreasing theirs. By moving in with the hands we recommend, you force the pros into coin-flip-type confrontations if they want to play, and that's just fine with you. You'll either have 13-10 the best of it or 13-10 the worst of it. From your standpoint, either one is far better than your overall expectation. These odds are close enough for luck to play a significant part in the outcome—a situation that suits you. The more you can relegate the outcome of a hand to the realm of a coin-flip, the more you'll neutralize the skill advantage of your more qualified opponents.

The Risks

Naturally, playing big-pot poker has inherent risks, but it's our contention that the potential rewards justify these risks. Sure, you may get knocked out earlier than you would have had you adopted a more cautious approach, but you'll also have a far greater chance of making the final table if you get lucky. To be successful with our approach, you must be willing, metaphorically, to risk dying at any moment. This takes courage. But your willingness to die is your strength. If you get knocked out, that's the breaks. You can play again tomorrow or next week. But when things go your way—when you knock out Johnny Chan and Phil Ivey, as Chris Moneymaker did at the 2003 WSOP main event—you'll forget the times you made an early exit. Simply put, in the early stages of your tournament career, our strategy gives you the best chance of winning. The risks come with the territory.

4

CHARACTERISTICS OF WINNING NO-LIMIT TOURNAMENT PLAYERS

You gotta have heart, miles and miles and miles of heart.

—*Damn Yankees*

Top-level NLH tournament players, to one degree or another, possess or exhibit the following characteristics:

- *Math skills*—Ability to apply math to decision-making.
- *Reading skills*—Ability to determine if a player is weak or strong based on observing betting patterns, mannerisms, demeanor, body language, etc.
- *Quick thinking*—Ability to make quick accurate decisions.
- *Patience*—Ability to wait for profitable situations to arise.
- *Discipline*—Ability to stick with a game plan.
- *Flexibility*—Ability to modify approach based on the

composition of players at the table and the relative chip status.

- *Awareness*—Constantly scanning opponents, looking for clues that assist in decision-making.
- *Equanimity*—Doesn't get angry or frustrated.
- *Soft focus*—Ability to make decisions based on absorbing a variety of environmental inputs without using discursive thinking or extensive analysis. This, when combined with the ability to pick up tells, as discussed later, is often incorrectly referred to as "intuition."
- *Aggression*—An attacking dominating style.
- *Heart*—The courage to make a decision and act on it.
- *Fearlessness*—The ability to commit all the chips, even though the result may be elimination. In other words, a willingness to go broke.

Many characteristics on this list are fine nuances that require innate ability, experience, and training to cultivate and develop. The last three on the list—aggression, heart, and a lack of fear of going broke—are easier to learn and are the paramount characteristics necessary to master the basic strategy we present in this book. Let's examine each of these three in more detail.

Aggression

Aggression is built into the basic strategy. If you follow it, you'll have an attacking style of play.

In poker, if no one ever folded and every hand was a showdown, the best hand would always win. But this isn't how the game is played. Because of the power of betting, it's often the case that the hand that would have won is folded at some point.

In his excellent book *The Theory of Poker*, David Sklansky points out that every time you get your opponent to do something different from what he would have done had he seen your cards, you've gained. Aggressive betting and raising often convince your opponent that you have the best hand, which may or may not be true. These tactics increase the chances that your competition will make mistakes. The fact that most confrontations are heads-up, and that your style of play usually forces a decision based on seeing only two cards, makes accurate decision-making especially difficult for your opponents. This is one of the pillars of the Kill Phil strategy. Undoubtedly, some of the times that your opponent folds, he'll have a better hand than you. Your aggressive betting drives him out. If he could see your cards, he'd make different decisions, such as calling more frequently. But if he doesn't, according to Sklansky's principle, you've accomplished your mission.

Another important related concept is that each time you pick up a pot, your stack increases. Usually, it's in small increments as you pick up the blinds and antes, but when you win an all-in confrontation, your chips may increase dramatically. Each such increase makes you more dangerous to the other players, who know you can eliminate them in just one hand. As their caution increases, your aggressive tactics become even more effective.

A player picks up AA, KK, QQ, JJ, or AK suited an average of only once every five rounds in a full game. This means there are lots of hands where no one has a big starting hand. Someone has to win these hands. That someone is typically the most aggressive player at the table. Often, there's one dominant player at the table. If the other players allow it, he'll pick up more than his fair share of blinds and antes, as well as post-flop pots.

Good players continue to pound on tight passive players. This is how they want you to be—civil, docile, and easy to control. If you want to win, your job is to make these players as unhappy as possible, and you do this by fighting aggression with aggression. Instead of allowing them to back you down, you put them to a guess for all their chips. They hate it! Look how upset Phil Hellmuth gets on TV when someone doesn't do what he wants him to do. In one WPT event, Antonio "the Magician" Esfandiari drove Phil absolutely crazy by consistently coming over the top of him when Phil raised pre-flop from late position. Antonio was supposed to be nice and fold like a good boy, but instead of following Phil's script, Antonio re-raised, literally driving Phil to distraction. You have to adopt the same tactics to win.

Anyone can have an extremely lucky run of cards. But even then, without aggression a stack eventually gets chewed up as the blinds and antes increase. A tight player with a good run of cards gathers some chips; an aggressive player with a good run of cards gathers a lot of chips.

To be successful, you must continue to attack throughout the tournament and be willing to go broke at any point in your effort to win. Ironically, the more you learn about no-limit hold 'em, the harder it may be to stay aggressive. Why? Because as your skill level increases, you realize that you play better than a significant number of your foes. Knowing that you can outplay others may persuade you to take fewer risks. You may ask yourself, "Why should I jeopardize all my chips before seeing the flop in this hand when I know I can pick up some easier pots later?" Like Phil Hellmuth, you may not want to risk all your chips without a lock, or close to it. This can serve to ameliorate your newly acquired aggressive tendencies. Knowledge can increase fear of loss, and this can be counterproductive. Several top players did better early in their careers when they knew less, but were more aggressive than they are now.

Although smoothing rough edges and continuing to refine your game is constructive, severely curtailing a fearless attacking game plan is undoubtedly an error. The Kill Phil advanced strategies teach you how to modulate and refine aggressiveness depending on the circumstances, while maintaining it as the primary weapon in your arsenal.

Heart

In this context, heart is synonymous with courage, and all great no-limit hold 'em players have heart. Whether it's a big call, a brazen bluff, or even a spectacular laydown, winning players have the courage of their convictions.

Although aggression is built into our strategy, it takes courage to follow through. You mustn't hesitate to pull the trigger when the strategy calls for it, even when you have a marginal hand. Chickening out, when you're supposed to make an all-in bet, can be costly.

You'll probably hear derogatory comments about your play from the Phils, or wannabe Phils. They do this to put you off your game, hoping you'll lose your nerve. They fire every arrow in their psychological quiver to get you to change your tactics. Stay the course! The more you follow the strategy, the more frustrated they'll become.

Not only does it take heart to stay aggressive, it's also required to *combat* aggression. As we've said, you've got to stand up to the bullies. Re-stealing takes guts. If you're called, you may be out on a limb, facing possible mortality. To win though, you must have the courage to take such risks. Tournament poker is not designed for the meek and faint-hearted!

Willingness to Go Broke

A willingness to go broke, and its corollary, fearlessness, is a hallmark of winning players. If you're not willing to risk busting out, you won't be able to reap the rewards of the strategy. Successful no-limit tournament players know that their chips are in jeopardy at all times, yet they're willing to put everything on the line if their judgment tells them the reward justifies the risk. At the 2005 WSOP main event, 5,618 players busted out. In that tournament, as in every standard-format tournament, only one player ultimately survives. Our strategy isn't designed to delay the pain of elimination for as long as possible. Leave that to the players content to die a lingering death. You need to accept the fact that you could get knocked out the first time you play a hand. The KP system recognizes the risks inherent in no-limit tournaments, and is built around the fact that to reach the mountaintop, you must walk out on a lot of ledges. Acceptance of this allows KP practitioners to keep firing. If they go out, it'll be with guns blazing.

Convincing your opponents that you're not scared of busting out can be intimidating. Your unpredictability and volatility keep them on edge, continually putting them to a guess and forcing them to make incorrect laydowns. If they're more afraid of busting out than you are, as they are most of the time, you have a distinct edge. It's like fighting a crazy man. Who knows what he'll do next? Who indeed? As the poker expression goes, "There's a fine line between genius and madness." We aim to keep you just inside this line.

Part Two

The Kill Phil
Beginner Strategies

5

THE BASIS FOR THE KILL PHIL STRATEGIES

The policy of being too cautious is the greatest risk of all.

—Jawaharlal Nehru

The History of "All-In" No-Limit Hold 'Em Poker

Doyle Brunson calls it "2-card hold 'em." Daniel Negreanu calls players using the method "move-in specialists" (MISs). We call them "Phil Killers." More and more players are using the all-in bet with great success. Chief among them are young Scandinavian players who seem to have adopted this tactic en masse. The concept isn't original. In 2002, David Sklansky expounded on an all-in strategy, which he dubbed the *System*, designed for a player who had never played before in *Tournament Poker for Advanced Players*.

The strategy presented in this book builds on what David and others have uncovered. We believe it's the shortest path to becoming an accomplished tournament player, while also being easy to implement in actual tournament play. We've also taken the strategy beyond the basics for new players, recommending advanced strategies that incorporate poker judgment that can be implemented as players gain experience. It targets players who are familiar with tournament poker, either through television, online play, or limited experience in traditional tournaments. A player who masters these concepts will be a threat in any tournament and should have the necessary foundation to advance to world-class status by continuing to play and study.

As the authors of this book, we've experienced firsthand the frustration of playing against opponents who employ the all-in tactic. Lee was at the final table in a no-limit tournament in Europe in which an unknown player seated to his immediate right pushed in all of his chips whenever the action got to him if no one else had entered the pot, regardless of his hand. For several rounds, no one held a hand they felt confident in challenging with, and this self-styled Phil Killer soon became the chip leader without ever showing a hand! He wound up finishing second. Lee finished fourth after getting knocked out by this player when he decided he had no choice but to make a stand with pocket 8s, and lost to T7 off-suit.

Recently, variations of this all-in style have even been implemented at the final table of WPT televised events. Hoyt Corkins drove Phil Hellmuth and Daniel Negreanu crazy in two separate WPT final-table appearances by repeatedly moving in. (Phil dubbed Hoyt "Mr. Move All-In.")

Lately, we've noticed increased numbers of discussions on this topic on poker Web sites. In one thread, a poster moaned about a player who moved all-in every hand whenever he got heads-up in a tournament. He derided the player, but this is clearly a sound strategy against a better player when the blinds and antes are high. In fact, it's our recommended Kill Phil basic strategy for heads-up final-table play.

No-limit hold 'em events are becoming progressively more popular. Bellagio has adopted a policy of strictly no-limit hold 'em events in all their upcoming tournaments. This is the game players see on TV and it's what they want to play. Casinos give players what they want, and that's no-limit hold 'em.

The Premise of the Kill Phil Beginner's Strategies

This book contains four versions of Kill Phil strategies: KP Rookie, KP Basic, KP Basic Plus, and KP Expert. The beginner's strategies, Rookie and Basic, are designed for the complete poker novice. They provide a method that, when learned and strictly applied, requires no decision-making. As has been explained, the backbone of all the KP strategies is the all-in bet. In most cases, this all-in move will be made pre-flop. As you progress, KP Basic Plus and KP Expert provide variations on style and a more advanced strategy, including some deviations from the all-in strategy, that allow you to modify your play as you become more proficient. These advanced adjustments make you less predictable and more difficult to read. But first, let's start with the basics.

There's a natural tendency for a new player to gravitate to the easiest-to-implement strategy, which is the KP Rookie. But be aware that this is truly an emergency strategy—a port in a storm, so to speak, if you find yourself in a position where you have to play right now or have a friend or spouse who wants to compete. You certainly won't have an advantage playing the strict KP Rookie, but neither will you be playing an absolute can't-win strategy.

We highly recommend that you learn the complete KP Basic, then progress as quickly as possible to the Basic Plus. This is the point at which you'll be a bona fide threat in almost any tournament you play. Later chapters cover KP Expert, which is the top of the Kill Phil ladder.

The Rookie strategy can be learned in less than an hour, whereas the full KP Basic will take roughly as long as it takes to learn an elemental winning strategy for black-jack. In KP Basic, how you play specified hands changes, depending on how many chips you have and the amount of the blinds and antes. Many will find this book's companion strategy cards a valuable aid in learning and implement-ing the strategy (see ad, back of book). Unlike blackjack, there are no casino restrictions regarding the use of pen-cil, paper, notebooks, or strategy cards at the poker table. Although you may feel a bit awkward breaking out your basic-strategy cue cards in the middle of a tournament, it's perfectly acceptable. If you prefer, you can simply refresh your memory by referring to them on breaks.

The KP Basic player is playing in a manner that greatly enhances his chances of success. Here are some of the rea-sons why it works.

• Hand selection is a key skill in no-limit hold 'em. The basic strategy picks your spots for you, based on your chip count and the cost of the blinds and antes per round.

• If you move in nearly every time you play a hand, you disguise the strength of your hand, which puts your opponents to a guess. Good players hate having to guess. No one will be able to judge the strength of your hand by the size of your bet.

• You frequently force players to lay down hands that

are better than yours, because they fear going broke. Each time you accomplish this, you're gaining and your opponents are losing.

• Experts use small-ball tactics to carve up a table. You'll refuse to fight the good players on their terms. Instead of small ball, you play long ball, forcing them to either back down or risk going broke.

• You often force experts into negative-EV situations. While you welcome a coin-flip, the more skilled opponents will back down, correctly looking for better spots.

• Your fearlessness will scare other players. The good player, who's used to controlling the game by bullying, will be pushed off this strategy. This levels the playing field. To illustrate, let's say everyone at the table used a KP-style strategy against one good player. The expert's tactics of picking up blinds and antes and outplaying his opponents after the flop would be nullified, because someone would be going all-in nearly every pot.

The players who'll be most hurt by this strategy are the best and most aggressive players—namely, the Phils.

The Fundamentals of the Beginner's Strategies

Picking up blinds, antes, and small pots is an art form for proficient players. It requires substantial quantities of good judgment and game experience. The experts use a variety of techniques to accomplish this goal. While beginners can't begin to compete at this level, they do have one weapon that trumps all the finesse moves—the big gun. Using only your all-in heavy artillery, you accomplish several things:

• By design, you attack the blinds, often even more aggressively than the pros.

• You prevent pros from re-raising and playing you off a hand.

• You need none of the knowledge and experience of the pros.

• You neutralize their advantage in judgment.

• You neutralize positional disadvantages.

• Your chances of being called are lessened, because your opponents must call a much bigger bet than usual, which jeopardizes a number of chips that exceeds their comfort level.

• You discourage players with medium hands from entering pots, due to their concern that you might re-raise all-in.

• When you do get called, your chances of being in a hand that's a huge underdog are lessened. You'll rarely be in a position where you're dominated. The hand groupings are devised with this goal in mind.

• You capitalize on a run of good luck.

If players know what you're doing, they'll be forced to call with less powerful hands. That's good. If they fold, that's even better. As a novice, you don't fear "races."

6

KILL PHIL ROOKIE

Keep it simple, stupid.
—KISS Method

The primary beginner's strategy, Kill Phil Basic, is powerful and relatively simple. But a reasonable amount of study and practice are necessary to become proficient in its application. What if you had to play a no-limit hold 'em tournament today? Say there's a drawing for a free entry into a tournament and your name is pulled. You're familiar with hold 'em, but you've never played in a tournament before. Can you compete? Probably not. At least not without help. So here it is.

Your main consideration in choosing your strategy is how much time you have to prepare. If you have a day or less, you have a problem. Sklansky's *System* proposes the following.

"For the first few levels raise or re-raise all-in with AA only; otherwise fold. After this, in unraised pots move in with any pair, AK, any suited ace, and suited connectors

down to 54 suited; otherwise fold. If a pot is raised before the action gets to you, move in with AA, KK, or AK
suited."

This extremely simplified approach gives an absolute
novice as good a chance as possible. With the exception
of adding KK to AA in the first few levels, we don't see a
better way to play, given the truncated nature of the advice. (We include KK, because we feel that the infusion of
Internet and more inexperienced players in today's tournaments makes it more likely than when Sklansky originally
devised the *System* that an all-in move could be called by
a player with hands as weak as AK, QQ, or worse.) We
recommend employing the more aggressive tactics (after
Sklansky's AA-only period) when the antes commence,
usually at the fourth or fifth level. In tournaments that
don't use antes at any point, start playing aggressively at
the fourth blind level.

While Sklansky didn't specifically address situations
when one or more players had limped (just called the
amount of the big blind), we interpret his intention to be
that an unraised pot with limpers is classified as an unraised pot. Regardless, in KP Rookie, that is our recommendation.

This bare-bones approach is surprisingly effective.
However, the player is left in the lurch in two areas that
Sklansky's *System* does not address: post-flop (when you're
still in the pot because no one raised prior to it) and play
at the final table.

Post-Flop

The only time you'll have to make a decision after the
flop is when you're in the big blind, no one raises pre-flop,
and you don't have a hand that meets the KP Rookie rais-

ing criteria. Given your very limited tournament experience as a new player, we've kept this strategy as simple as possible.

If you flop 2-pair, 3-of-a-kind, a set, a straight, a flush, a full house, 4-of-a-kind, or a straight flush, move all-in when it's your turn to act; otherwise check, and fold if there's a bet. The one caveat is that the 2-pair must use two cards from your hand that match two cards on the board. A hand such as 97 with a flop of 9-7-2 qualifies; a hand such as TT with a flop of 9-9-2 doesn't. If everyone checks on the flop, you get a free look at the turn card.

The turn—The same parameters apply. Move in if you've now made 2-pair or better; otherwise check and fold if someone bets.

There's a caveat here, too: If the board shows 4 cards to either a straight or a flush and you don't have the top card that makes the straight or flush, check and fold to any bet. Also, if you've made a straight, but there's a 4-flush on board, check and fold if someone bets. If no one bets, you'll get to see the river card.

The river—The same precepts that guided you on the turn apply to the river—move in with 2-pair or better, unless there's either a 4-card straight or flush on the board. If there is, follow the same guidelines as above.

As soon as you're ready, we encourage you to move up to the KP Basic post-flop strategy, which plugs some of the inevitable holes that accompany a simplified version such as this.

Final Table

Should you be fortunate enough to make it to the final table, don't panic. Continue to use the KP Rookie strategy until you're down to 4- to 6-handed.

4- to 6-handed—In unraised pots, go all-in with the usual hands, plus A7 unsuited or better, KT unsuited or better, and 1-gap suited connectors 64s and above. In raised pots, re-raise all-in with all pairs 66 and higher and any hand of AT or higher. Otherwise fold.

3-handed—In unraised pots, move-in with any pair, any ace, any king, and any suited connector that includes a 6 or higher, including those with one or two gaps, such as 85s, 74s, etc., down to 63s. In raised pots, re-raise all-in with any pair, A7 offsuit or better, KJ or better, and any suited ace. Otherwise fold.

Heads-up—Move in every hand.

If you don't lose your nerve and don't deviate from the system, you might be surprised at what happens. If talk of a deal arises, refer to "Deals" (pg. 168) for guidance.

As discussed, you should be able to commit the strategy to memory in about an hour. However, you could also use the Kill Phil strategy cards, which are a condensed outline of all the Kill Phil strategies and include Rookie, to help you (or simply jot down the above strategy and use it as a guide).

7

KILL PHIL BASIC

I'm going to call you, because I know if I don't you're going to just keep moving in every hand.
—Daniel Negreanu to Hoyt
Corkins at the WPT final table of
the PokerStars Caribbean Adventure

Kill Phil Basic is the foundational strategy in the KP hierarchy. Basic differs from Rookie in several ways, but primarily in the fact that here, we consider our relative strength at a given time in a tournament via two important indicators: the "cost-per-round" (CPR) and the "chip-status index" (CSI). We also consider position and the action of our opponents when choosing the hands we play and the actions we take with them.

THE CPR AND CSI

In no-limit tournaments, correct Kill Phil strategy changes due to the increasing blind and ante structure, along with changes in the size of your bankroll. As you play, it's important to have a handle on how big your bankroll is relative to the blinds. Do you have a huge stack, big stack, medium stack, or small stack? We compare the cost to play per round to our chip count to make this determination, which is quantified by the chip-status index, or CSI.

In order to determine the CSI, you must first know the cost-per-round, or CPR. This is the total amount of blinds and antes you have to put up to play around the table one time. Once the cost-per-round is determined, it can be compared to your chip total to define which part of the strategy you use.

Calculating the CPR

The cost-per-round is easy to calculate. Simply add the amount of the small blind and the big blind, plus the ante (when there is one) multiplied by the number of players at the table. In the early goings, there are usually no antes, so the CPR is the sum of the small and big blinds.

For example, if the blinds are 25-50, the CPR is 75. When the blinds are 100-200, the CPR is 300. And when the blinds are 300-600, the CPR is 900.

When an ante is instituted in later rounds, the CPR must include this cost, plus the player multiplier. In a situation where the blinds are 200-400 with a 50 ante, the CPR for 10-handed play is 200 + 400 + (50 x 10) = 1,100.

Calculating the CSI

The chip-status index is the important indicator you must have to gauge your current strength in a tournament and determine which part of the KP strategy should be employed. The CSI is calculated by multiplying the CPR by key numbers and comparing the product to your chip count.

The key numbers are 4, 10, and 30. Multiplying the CPR by these numbers gives you a whole-number indicator that can be easily compared to your chip count to derive your CSI. The greater the multiple that your stack exceeds, the stronger position you're in. For example, if your chip count exceeds 30X the CPR, you're in best position with a "huge" stack.

The points of demarcation are as follows:

CSI	Chip Count
Huge stack	exceeds 30X CPR
Big stack	exceeds 10X CPR
Medium stack	exceeds 4X CPR
Small stack	is below 4X CPR

At the beginning of a typical big-buy-in tournament, everyone at the table has a huge stack. Take the start of the World Series of Poker, where everyone begins with 10,000 and the blinds are 25-50 with no ante. On the opening hand, there's 25 + 50 = 75 in the pot. Multiplying 75 by 30 gives you 2,250, which is greatly exceeded by your 10,000 starting chip count. You have a huge stack. Note that had there been a 25 ante in a 10-player game, the CPR would have been 325 and multiplying by 30 would yield 9,750, still a huge stack.

As you play, your chip count will vacillate and the blinds will increase, necessitating that you recalculate the

CSI frequently. Let's say that later in the tournament the blinds have increased to 100-200 and your chip count has dropped to 8,300. The CPR is now 300 and 30 x 300 is 9,000. You're now below the 30-multiple threshold, so you multiply again using the next highest key number, which is 10. Since 300 x 10 is only 3,000, you're easily in big-stack territory. Had your chip count been below 3,000, you would then multiply the CPR of 300 by 4 to determine if you had a medium stack (above 1,200) or a small stack (below 1,200).

Once you're into the tournament, you can use an easier two-step process to determine your CSI. After calculating the CPR, multiply first by 10, which will tell you if you're a big stack or below. If your stack exceeds the 10X figure, you can multiply the first calculation again by 3 to determine easily if you qualify as a huge stack. If your stack is below 10X the CPR, then multiply the CPR by 4 to find out if you're medium (above 4X) or small (below).

Example: The blinds are 150-300 and there's a 100 ante. The CPR is 1,450 and you have about 11,000 in chips (rounding is OK). Multiplying 1,450 by 10 indicates that you don't have a big stack (14,500 is greater than 11,000). Now multiply 1,450 by 4. It's OK to make it easy by calculating 4 x 1,500. Since your chip count is greater than 6,000, you now have a medium stack. Much later in the tournament, let's say the structure is now 800-1,600/300 and you have 18,000 in chips. The CPR is 5,400, so you obviously don't have a big stack (10 x 5,400 = 54,000, which is more than the amount of your chips), so multiply by 4. Again, round up if you like and the calculation is 4 x 5,500 = 22,000—your chip count is below this number, so you now have a small stack.

The CSI alone is all you need to determine which part of the strategy you use.

THE HAND GROUPINGS

The hand groupings are plugged into a formula with the CSI to derive the playing strategy. (These groupings were selected to complement our move-in strategy and don't mimic the power rankings of other authors, which consider different factors.)

If you move in and don't get called, the cards you have don't matter. But when you do get called, you have a much better chance of winning a showdown if the cards in your hand are "live." Live cards are those that don't appear in your opponent's hand. If one of your cards is duplicated and your foe's other card is higher than yours, you're nearly a 3-1 underdog to win, when all the cards are out. This is called being "dominated."

For example, AK dominates AQ and wins a little less than 75% of the time. It's for this reason that hands such as AQ and KQ are rated lower than you might expect. The ten hand groups are (s = suited):

1) AA, KK
2) QQ, AKs, AK
3) JJ, TT, 99
4) AQs, 88 through 66
5) AQ, AJs, ATs
6) Suited connectors KQs through 54s
7) AJ, AT, KQ
8) 55 through 22, A9s through A2s, A9 through A7, KJs, KJ, KTs
9) 1-gap suited connectors QTs through 64s, A6 through A2
10) 2-gap suited connectors Q9s through 63s, K9s through K7s, Q8s, KT, QT, JT, K9, QJ

THE VALUE OF SUITED CONNECTORS

Suited connectors are a unique class of hands. When you move in in unraised pots, they'll often take the pot uncontested (as will any two cards). But in those rare instances when you're called, connectors are stronger than most players think.

When you make an all-in move, you'll generally get called by big pairs or AK. In this situation, you'd rather have a hand like 7♣6♣ than a hand such as AQ when your opponent has AK. Similarly, the 76 suited is better than JJ when your opponent has an overpair.

Suited connectors are unlikely to be dominated, which means that both your cards are likely to be "live." A♣K♦ is nearly a 3-1 favorite over A♥Q♠, but it's only 7-5 against 5♣4♣!

A pair is a favorite against two unsuited overcards. For example, 8♥8♦ is about a 12.5-10 favorite over A♠K♣. But trade in that AK for J♣T♣ and you're almost exactly even money against those two red 8s!

In pair-versus-pair confrontations, you're in bad shape if you have the underpair—about a 4.5-1 dog. Suited connectors fare better. The J♣T♣ is about a 3.6-1 underdog to two red aces, and 5♣6♣, 6♣7♣, and 7♣8♣ are all about 3.3-1 dogs.

In the late stages of a tournament, especially in short-handed play, some players play most Ax hands. If you make a move short-handed with suited connectors and happen to get called by a weak ace, you're in better shape than you might think. A♣6♥ is a mere 11-10 favorite over 8♦7♦. Compare this to a more common, but less attractive, alternative: A♠J♣ is 3-2 over K♦Q♥. The 8♦7♦ fares slightly better here too, despite the fact that both cards are lower than the AJ, being only a 7-5 dog. We'll take the suited connectors.

You should now understand why we rank suited connectors in NLH higher than hands such as AJ, AT, and KQ. However, suited connectors fare less well against a raise, especially one from late position. In this circumstance, when players can be raising with almost anything, we prefer big cards to suited connectors. The basic strategy considers this difference between unraised and raised pots. With suited connectors, we like to be the raiser, not the caller.

PLAYING ACES OR KINGS EARLY WITH SMALL BLINDS AND A LARGE STACK

It's important to emphasize that Kill Phil players are most vulnerable early in a tournament. This is particularly true of major tournaments, both live and online, when the blinds generally start out as a low percentage of starting stacks and playing levels last longer than in small-buy-in events.

Our strategy of avoiding small-ball situations makes the play of aces and kings a special case. The dilemma is that if you fail to raise enough with aces or kings, which are the only hands you'll be playing at the earliest levels, skilled players will be getting the correct odds to call and take a flop with speculative hands, such as pairs or suited connectors, hoping to break you if they make their hand and you commit the rest of your chips on the flop. You could simply move in pre-flop, but you're unlikely to get any action on your top pairs and will just win the relatively meaningless blinds.

What to do? Going all-in is certainly the safest route and you may catch an inexperienced opponent who's willing to put in all his chips with a lesser hand, such as QQ or AK. We've seen it happen. At the $15,000-entry WPT event at Bellagio in 2004, a player put in all his chips preflop with AK on the first deal of the tournament. Naturally, another player had AA. Taking such a risk was so surprising that the player with the aces screamed at him, "What are you doing?!"

Another option is to try to induce an opponent to make a mistake. Starting with a pair, the odds against flopping a set are 7.5-1. Given this, the simple solution is to make your initial raise large enough to make it incorrect (unprofitable) for an opponent to call. You can accomplish this, in an unopened pot, by betting about one-sixth of your stack. If you have the biggest stack of anyone yet to act, one-sixth of the biggest stack of players remaining in the hand also works. This needn't be exact. If called, move in on the flop. Folding your aces after the flop would be a very difficult judgment play, especially at this point in your tournament education. By doing anything other than moving in, you're opening yourself up to getting outplayed by a more experienced opponent.

As you can see, if your pre-flop bet is called, the caller gets the wrong price to take a flop. Anytime someone calls when they're getting the wrong price, they're making a mistake and their loss is your gain. For example, in the WSOP main event, each player starts with 10,000 in chips and the blinds are 25-50. In this situation, an initial raise to around 1,500 will give the speculators the wrong price to call. At the WPT Championship event, players start with 30,000 and blinds of 100-200. Following the formula, a raise to around 5,000 would make calling incorrect. In the weekly PokerStars online tournament, the starting stack is 2,500 with 10-20 blinds. Here, an initial raise to 400 would be about right. Online, large raises like this aren't so unusual and you might be really fortunate online and have someone with QQ, JJ, or AK move in on you. At any rate, you'll discourage hands from entering that could break you post-flop.

If you make the recommended raise with kings and get called, what should you do if an ace flops? This is a tough situation for a player of any skill level. Simply moving in is okay. You may be beat, but as an inexperienced player, you don't want to start playing guessing games. If you want to consider other options, the question to consider is, what did your opponent have to call, and not re-raise, pre-flop? He could be trapping with aces. He could also have kings. Queens, jacks, and AK are other, though less likely, possibilities. If your opponent acts first and makes a significant bet, you're probably beat and should consider folding. If he checks to you, bet about 75% of the size of the pot. It would be hard for him to continue without having you beat. If you act first, about 75% of the pot is a good bet here, too. If he calls or raises, you should assume you're beat. If you've been called, stop betting and try to check the rest of the way, but fold if your opponent bets. If you're raised on the flop, fold. This discussion illustrates the complexities of post-flop play, which is why the Kill Phil strategy avoids post-flop play as much as possible.

If you have kings and happen to run into aces, you've gotten unlucky and are probably going to get busted. While it's possible to lay down kings (see "Folding Kings," pg. 141), we don't recommend it for new players, unless you've made less than an all-in bet and an ace flops, as in the example above. If the thought of running into aces and getting broke very early in a tournament really bothers you, limit your play at the earliest levels to aces only.

As you become more skilled, you'll undoubtedly become more sophisticated in your play of aces. Additional options are presented in the advanced-play sections of the book.

POSITION

Position is important, because the later you act, the more information you gather from the actions of your opponents who act before you and, in unopened pots, the less likely it becomes that there's a big hand out there. Accordingly, the later your position, the more you can expand your list of starting hands.

Additionally, early-position raisers are to be more feared than late-position raisers, because your opponents are likely to also be adjusting their hand requirements according to position. Therefore, your re-raising hand requirements expand versus late-position raisers. The strategy accounts for these factors.

As used in Kill Phil, position relates to the order in which a player is forced to act pre-flop. The first player to act (and the one with worst position) is considered to be the player to the left of the big blind. We break down the positions and assign numbers according to the order below. The lower the number, the better the betting position pre-flop (post-flop, the button has the best betting position). Note that the designations move counter-clockwise starting from the big blind:

big blind	1
small blind	2
button	3
cutoff	4
middle position	5, 6, and 7
early position	8, 9, and 10

Numbering the positions in this manner makes it easy to adjust for any number of players, with the adjustments occurring automatically. If there are only seven players, for example, the 5, 6, and 7 positions still use the middle-position strategy. In such cases, even though seats 5, 6, and 7 are technically in early position, the middle-position strategy applies in this short-handed game. The cutoff would use the cutoff strategy, regardless of the number of players, and so on.

After the flop, the first remaining player to the left of the button acts first. In KP Basic, the only time you'd be involved post-flop would be if you were in the big blind and no one raised (at this point from the small blind, we recommend either moving in or folding), or if you made a less than all-in bet with aces or kings.

In "Variations to Basic Strategy" (pg. 96), we cover some other situations where a player might get involved post-flop, including calling from the small blind. For post-flop play, refer to "Basic Post-Flop Play" (pg. 83).

STRATEGY FOR KILL PHIL BASIC

All guidelines refer to play before the flop. If your hand doesn't fall into the category listed, the play is to fold. "Late position" refers to the cutoff and button only.

Before getting into the specific strategy, a quick reminder of the dangers of playing a huge stack early is in order. The larger a player's stack size compared to the blinds, the more complex no-limit hold 'em becomes. This is the situation in most cash games, for which the Kill Phil strategy isn't well-suited. The reason the Kill Phil strategy is effective in tournaments is that the escalation of the blinds forces play to a point where the blinds are high in relation to the average stack. In the early stages of a tournament, however, play is more like a ring game, with all its inherent complexities. This is especially true in the major tournaments that have large starting stacks compared to the blinds and longer time intervals at each limit. These tournaments are the toughest for Kill Phil players, because it takes longer than in smaller tournaments, or in online tournaments, to get to the point where the strategy is most effective.

As discussed at length earlier, KP players are vulnerable early in tournaments, when all players have very large stacks. We're well aware that many players have a hard time sitting through several levels playing few, if any, hands. However, the purpose of the KP strategy is to keep inexperienced players away from situations in which they're out-gunned by more experienced pros who feed on newer players who don't have the experience to stay out of trouble. It's beyond the scope of this book to deal with all the intricacies of post-flop play in no-limit hold 'em tournaments. Becoming proficient in the post-flop arena requires talent and many hours at the tables. Unless you've already developed the talent to swim with the sharks, you're better off staying where it's safe.

At the very early stages, especially in major tournaments, the CSI for everyone is very high. Risking your entire stack with less than the best hands for the small rewards to be gained by stealing the blinds at this time is incorrect.

Playing a Huge Stack
(chip count > 30X the CPR)

In unraised pots (from any position)—
If there are limpers: Move in with Group 1

With no limpers: Move in with Group 1
                               or
                               Bet about one-sixth of your
                               stack size. If re-raised, move
                               in. Post-flop, move in re-
                               gardless of the flop, unless
                               you have kings and an ace
                               flops (see "Playing Aces
                               or Kings Early with Small
                               Blinds and a Large Stack,"
                               pg. 73).

In single-raised pots—
With Group 1, re-raise five times the amount of the raise or one-sixth of your stack size, whichever is greater. If this computation is too difficult to figure, move in. If a non-all-in bet is re-raised, move in. Post-flop, move in regardless of what flops.

If multiple raises—
Move in with Group 1, otherwise fold.

Playing a Big Stack
(chip count > 10X the CPR)

In unraised pots—

Early position	
with limpers:	Move in with Group 1
if no limpers:	With Group 1, move in or Bet about one-sixth of your stack size. If re-raised, move in. Post-flop, move in regardless of the flop, unless you have kings and an ace flops (see "Playing Aces or Kings Early with Small Blinds and a Large Stack," pg. 73).
Middle position:	With Group 1, play the same way as above. Move in with Group 2
Cutoff:	Move in with Groups 1-4
Button:	Move in with Groups 1-8
Either blind:	Move in with Groups 1-10 (except with early-position limper; see "Variations to Basic Strategy" #3, pg. 96)

> **Key Point:** The fewer the remaining players, the greater your chances of stealing the blinds. This effect is magnified when only a few players are left to act. This is why your raising requirements loosen significantly as your position improves and there are only one or two players left to act.

In raised pots—

Early position raiser:	Move in with Group 1
Middle-position raiser:	Move in with Groups 1-2
Late-position raiser:	Move in with Groups 1-3
Small blind raiser:	Move in with Groups 1-3

If multiple raises—

Move in with Group 1, otherwise fold.

Playing a Medium Stack
(chip count > 4X the CPR)

In unraised pots (limpers OK)—

Early position:	Move in with Groups 1-5
Middle position:	Move in with Groups 1-6
Cutoff:	Move in with Groups 1-8
Button, either blind:	Move in with Groups 1-10

In raised pots—

Early-position player raiser:	
	Move in with Groups 1-2
Middle-position player raiser:	
	Move in with Groups 1-5
Late-position raiser:	Move in with Groups 1-5 and 7
Small-blind raiser:	Move in with Groups 1-5, 7, and 8

Notice that the value of suited connectors goes down in raised pots. Also, for calling purposes, KQ suited should be treated the same as KQ off-suit, since it obviously makes no sense to raise with KQ off-suit (Group 7), but not with KQ suited.

If multiple raises—
Move in with Group 1; otherwise fold.

Playing a Small Stack
(chip count < 4X the CPR)

In unraised pots (limpers OK)—
Early position: Move in with Groups 1-7
Middle position: Move in with Groups 1-8
Cutoff, button, and either blind:
                           Move in with Groups 1-10

In raised pots—
Early-position raiser: Move in with Groups 1-4
Middle-position raiser: Move in with Groups 1-5 and 7*
Late-position raiser: Move in with Groups 1-5, 7, and 8
Small blind raiser: Move in with Groups 1-5, 7, and 8

*KQ suited should be treated the same, as already explained.

If multiple raises—
Move-in with groups 1-2, otherwise fold.

Playing Against an All-In Bet

In virtually every tournament, there are times when an opponent makes an all-in bet and you're faced with a decision. Often, the all-in player has fewer chips than you. Here are some basic strategy guidelines.

• Use the same criteria that you'd use for a raised pot and move in over the top of the all-in raiser if your hand qualifies. In other words, bet all the chips you have, even if you have more chips than your opponent's all-in wager.

• If there's been both a raise and an all-in re-raise prior to the action getting to you, move in with aces or kings only, unless you're a small stack, in which case move in with Groups 1-2; otherwise fold.

BASIC POST-FLOP PLAY

The flop is a key strategic point in a hold 'em hand, assuming the players involved still have chips to bet. Correct post-flop play is highly complex and the area in which expert players derive their greatest advantage. As a beginner, it would be nice if you could avoid butting heads in this area altogether, but at times you'll need a post-flop strategy.

Playing the basic strategy, you'll find yourself involved in a hand post-flop when you raise less than all-in and get called or when you're the big blind and no one raises. Use the following post-flop rules.

• If you raise less than all-in pre-flop and get called by one or more players, see the discussion in "Playing Aces or Kings Early with Small Blinds and a Large Stack" (pg. 73).

• If you're in the big blind, get a free flop, and flop a full house, 4-of-a-kind, or a straight flush, check, then raise all-in if someone bets. If no one bets, bet half your chips on the turn or raise all-in if someone bets before you. If called, bet the rest of your stack on the river.

If you flop top pair with top kicker, an overpair, 2-pair with an unpaired board, 3-of-a-kind, a set, a straight, or a flush, bet or raise all-in. (Note that there's a distinction between "3-of-a-kind" and a "set" in that with a set, you have a concealed pair in your hand). With all other hands, check and fold if your opponent bets.

If there's a bet and a raise before it gets to you, move in with a set, or better, regardless of the texture of the flop. Also move-in with top 2-pair if the flop doesn't contain three consecutive cards or three cards of the same suit. If you flop 3-of-a-kind, move in if you have top kicker in your hand. For example, move in with A7, if the flop is 7-7-T. With the same flop, fold 74 to a bet and a raise. With all other hands, check and fold if there's a bet.

The above guidelines are simplistic, but for the novice, they're in keeping with our goal of avoiding complicated decisions. When there are antes as well as blinds, you may want to add more punch to the basic strategy. To do so (in addition to the above), move in about half the time that you flop an open-ended straight or a 4-card flush draw and there's been no action when it gets to you, provided that both cards in your hand are required to make the straight or flush. For example, you might consider moving in if you have 98 in the big blind and the board reads 6-7-2. But you should never do so if you have 94 and the board reads 6-7-8. Rather than randomizing this decision, select the times when you have two overcards to the board with your straight or flush draw, the nut flush draw, or a pair in addition your flush draw or open-end top-straight draw, to move in. The times when you check your draw, fold if your opponent bets. If he checks, move in on the turn if you make the straight or flush.

FINAL TABLE

If you get to this point, your style of play has worked well. Don't abandon the strategy now. The players at the final table will generally be good players. If you're inexperienced, continuing to follow the strategy is your best chance. We don't present an advanced final-table strategy, per se, in this book; however, the strategy below is very powerful. As you gain in experience, your poker judgment will point you to areas where you can profitably deviate.

This strategy also applies if your table becomes short-handed, such as when there are two or three tables left.

Until You Get Down to 6-Handed

Use the normal strategy. Remember to use the adjustments for position as described in "Position" (pg. 76). For instance, if 7-handed, the first player to act is 7, and should use the middle-position strategy. If you've mastered the KP Plus or KP Expert concepts presented later in the text, integrate them into your play.

4- to 6-Handed

Increasing limits combined with blinds coming around more quickly necessitate increased aggression.

With a Huge Stack—In an unraised pot, move in with Groups 1-5, unless there's a first-position limper, in which case move in with Groups 1-3; otherwise fold. If there's an early-position limper, calling with Group 4-6 hands is also an option, provided you follow the recommended post-flop strategy or have developed a good feel for post-flop play. In raised pots, re-raise all-in with Groups 1-3; otherwise fold.

With a Big Stack—In unraised pots, move in with Group 1-7 hands, unless there's an early-position limper, in which case move in with Groups 1-3; otherwise fold. Calling as discussed above is also a viable option. In raised pots, re-raise all-in with Groups 1-4; otherwise fold.

With a Medium Stack—In all unraised pots, move in with Group 1-8 hands. In raised pots, re-raise all-in with Groups 1-5.

With a Small Stack—In all unraised pots, move in with Group 1-10 hands. In raised pots, move in with any pair or any ace with a kicker ten or higher.

3-Handed

Assuming you're inexperienced, it's in your best interest to try to make a deal at almost any point at the final table (see "Deals," pg. 168), even if you have to take a little the worst of it. Failing this, with a medium or larger stack, move in with Groups 1-10 in all unraised pots. In raised pots, re-raise all-in with Groups 1-8, except Group 6 (KQs is OK). If you're a small stack, move in every hand in an unraised pot. In a raised pot, consider folding the weakest 10% of hands (see next page).

Heads-Up

Give your opponent his last chance to make a deal. Failing this, show him no mercy and move in every hand!

Radical, But Effective

This heads-up strategy works no matter what the relationship is between you and your opponents' stacks. For example, down to two players in a nationally televised

WPT event, Dewey Tomko, with 700,000, used this exact strategy against Paul Phillips, who had 5,000,000. After about eight hands, Dewey had built up to around 1,500,000, as a noticeably frustrated Phillips folded each time. Then Dewey moved in with Q8 and Paul called with pocket 7s. A 7 flopped and Dewey was out. Dewey was a slight underdog on that last hand, but had he gotten lucky, the chip count would have been even.

Does this strategy sound radical? Maybe. But the fact is that in a heads-up match between you and an expert where you both have stacks equal to 17 times the blinds and antes, by using this strategy you are, at worst, a 3-2 dog if he plays optimally. If you both have fewer chips, your chance of winning gets even better. If you both have only five times the amount of the blinds and antes, the best the greatest Phil in the world can do with an optimal strategy is only slightly better than even money. And if he doesn't know the optimal defense, you're a favorite! The reason for this is that each time he folds, your stack size increases. And once you've passed him in chips, even if he calls and wins, you won't be busted, but he'll be out if he loses.

One variation for the heads-up strategy is to eliminate some of the weakest hands from those you play. If you fold or just check in the big blind if he calls the small blind, with off-suit 73, 63, 53, 43, 82, 72, 62, 42, and 32, you eliminate about 10% of hands and keep your opponents guessing about what you're doing. Keeping them off balance adds to their frustration and uncertainty about how to defend against you.

Credit for proving the optimal result for heads-up play, where one player moves in every hand, goes to Paul Pudaite. In a superb post on rec.gambling.poker in 1996, Paul showed that if each player has 10 chips and the blinds are 1-2, the optimal defense against a player moving in every hand will make the defender only a 51% favorite if he starts in the big blind and a 52% favorite if he starts in the small blind. If each player starts with 50 chips and the blind structure is the same, the optimal defense will win about 59% of the time if the defender starts in the big blind and around 61% of the time if he starts in the small blind. If you fold a few hands or if your opponent plays sub-optimally (which is likely), these odds are reduced. Remember this when negotiating a deal when heads-up.

SIT-N-GO TOURNAMENTS AND SINGLE-TABLE SATELLITES

Single-table Sit-n-Go events (SNGs) are essentially one-table tournaments. They're tremendously popular at online sites, because players can participate in a quick tournament whenever time permits.

One-table live-play satellites are popular at big tournaments, because they offer players a chance to gain entry into a big event at a reduced price. They differ from SNGs in that there's generally only one winner, while SNGs often pay the top three finishers. Both SNGs and one-table satellites are similar to playing at a final table, except that everyone starts out with an equal amount of chips. The good news is that you don't need to learn a separate strategy for each case. Our final-table strategy works in all of them.

But be forewarned—your opponents won't like your strategy. Online, you're likely to be subjected to abusive language from the other players. Words such as "idiot," "moron," and "pathetic" will probably be hurled your way. One of our testers provided empirical verification of the validity of the final-table strategy in SNGs by playing hundreds of online matches. While he was satisfied with the application, he was also amazed at how outraged other players became over his tactics and how they let it affect their play. As a rule, opponents began by playing too tight against him. They became progressively more frustrated as his tactic became obvious, not knowing how to combat it. Some players became so flustered that they made costly mistakes, calling all-in bets with hands that were almost certain to be underdogs.

In heads-up play, his tactic of moving all-in every hand was regularly the target of maximal derision from his opponents. "This isn't poker," his opponents would write (in between the less kindly epithets). In fact, they had a point. This isn't poker, at least not in the traditional sense. It's tournament poker. As we've told you throughout this book, tournament strategy differs from normal poker strategy. Players who have difficulty grasping this most likely also have problems succeeding in the tournament arena. If players could easily exploit Kill Phil practitioners, they'd simply keep quiet and rake in the chips. The fact that they voice their complaints is further testimony to the effectiveness of the strategy.

SNGs are a simple way to get your feet wet in tournament play. Online, you can play for just about any stakes you want. It's also a great way to practice the final-table strategy. Don't let your opponents' remarks bother you. Their frustration and resulting mistakes accrue to your benefit. Turn off your chat and fire away!

Key Point: The final-table tournament strategy can effectively be used for playing SNGs.

ONLINE PLAY

Online play is generally considerably looser than live play. We attribute this to the enormous number of players with limited experience who are now playing online. Fields are huge and still growing. More than 2,000 starters regularly appear in the weekly $200-buy-in tournament on PokerStars and numbers well in excess of 1,000 players turn out for the big weekend tournaments at other sites.

Due to lower standards for online play, strategy adjustments are necessary. One important difference is that big bets are more likely to be called. This means that you'll get paid off more frequently with big starting hands, such as aces or kings. For this reason, we don't recommend raising one-sixth of your stack with those hands. Just move in. Pocket queens are more likely to get called by lesser hands, such as JJ, TT, or worse. We've seen players over-call after an all-in bet and a call with pocket 3s! Ace-king is also more valuable online, as players often call a huge bet with hands such as AQ or worse.

Adjustments must be made in the online strategy for suited connectors. We don't rate them as highly online, since big bets with these hands pre-flop are more likely to get called. With these thoughts in mind, here's our recommended basic strategy for online play.

ONLINE BASIC STRATEGY

Playing a Big or Huge Stack
(chip count > 10X the CPR)

In unraised pots (limpers OK)—
Early and middle position:

	Move in with Groups 1-2
Late position:	Move in with Groups 1-3
Either blind:	Move in with Groups 1-5

In raised pots—
Early- or middle-position raiser:

	Move in with Groups 1-2
Late-position raiser:	Move in with Groups 1-3
Small-blind raiser:	Move in with Groups 1-4

Playing a Medium Stack
(chip count > 4X the CPR)

In unraised pots—

Early position:	Move in with Groups 1-5
Middle position:	Move in with Groups 1-7
Late position:	Move in with Groups 1-8
Either blind:	Move in with Groups 1-8

In raised pots—

Early-position raiser:	Move in with Groups 1-3
Middle-position raiser:	Move in with Groups 1-5 and 7

| Late-position raiser: | Move in with Groups 1-5 and 7 |
| Small-blind raiser: | Move in with Groups 1-5 and 7 |

Playing a Short Stack
(chip count < 4X the CPR)

In unraised pots—

Early position:	Move in with Groups 1-7
Middle position:	Move in with Groups 1-8
Late position and either blind:	
	Move in with Groups 1-10

In raised pots—

Early-position raiser:	Move in with Groups 1-5
Middle-position raiser:	Move in with Groups 1-5 and 7
Late-position raiser:	Move in with Groups 1-5, 7, and 8
Small-blind raiser:	Move in with Groups 1-5, 7, and 8

HOW TO AVOID TELLS

Expert players are superb at picking up on small nuances or changes in the demeanor of their adversaries, which are known as "tells." They hone this ability over time by carefully observing thousands of pressure-filled situations. They pride themselves on this ability and they should, because they're good! In fact, if you're not prepared, it's their main weapon against you as a Kill Phil player. So what's a novice to do?

The key is to act exactly the same no matter what you have. The more regimented you are, the fewer clues you'll provide. Here's what we suggest.

• Memorize your hand, including suits. Even when you have a pair, commit the suits to memory. If three of a suit flop and you peek at your cards because you can't remember if one of your cards is that suit, your sharp opponents will notice and act accordingly. Don't give them the opportunity. Do whatever it takes to indelibly inscribe your starting hand in your mind's eye.

• Always put a chip on your cards after you've looked at your hand. If you fold, remove the chip and push your cards away. If you intend to fold, don't give any indication of that until it's your turn to act. Indicating that you're going to fold isn't fair to the other players. Also, you don't want to alert your observant foes of your intention to play when you don't act as if you're going to fold. Stay focused and give no clues as to your intentions until it's your turn to act.

• If you're going to move in, pick a spot on the table to stare at and count to 15 slowly (not out loud, though). You might want to say to yourself "one thousand one, one thousand two," etc. until you reach 15. Then look at the dealer and clearly say, "All-in." Then find that same spot on the table and focus on it, keeping your face and body as relaxed as possible. Make sure you don't forget to breathe. Breathe normally and slowly. No matter what your opponent does or says, continue to focus on that spot. Meditate on it. Lose yourself completely in that lovely little piece of green felt. Let it absorb you. Don't sigh, cough, or twitch. Just try to be as relaxed and focused as possible. Your wily adversary may try to get you to laugh, talk, or react. You're above all that. Ignore him completely. Stay focused and keep breathing. A common ploy of battle-worn veterans is to ask, "How much have you got?" The reason they're asking isn't for information about your stack size, which they're more than capable of accurately gauging, but rather to pick up a tell. Phil Hellmuth is notorious for this. Don't answer and don't count your chips. Simply push your chips out a little and the dealer will count them for your opponent. This way, you'll give him no information.

We recommend wearing dark sunglasses, a broad brimmed hat or baseball cap, and a high-collared jacket or turtleneck as your standard tournament gear. The cap and glasses hide your eyes and the high collar covers your neck. Hiding your eyes helps mask your emotions. The high collar covers your carotid artery (sometimes incorrectly referred to as your "neck vein"). This is important, because when you have a weak hand, fear may cause a shot of adrenaline to rush into your system and your carotid neck pulse may start pumping wildly. Covering up these telltale signs leaves your astute opponents clueless.

THE TRANSITION TO BASIC PLUS

Using Downtime to Learn

By using proper basic strategy, not only do you become a threat with a reasonable expectation of success, you also gain real-time tournament experience. Use your time at the table to carefully observe the good players and to assimilate as much as possible.

Get a feel for the pace of play at your table. Notice the difference between play at a table filled with conservative players and one dominated by one or more aggressive pros.

Watch for physical tells and observe the betting patterns of each contestant. Do they slow-play big hands? Do they either over-bet or under-bet with marginal holdings? While observing, see if you can guess a player's hand. Make notes, either mental or written, on how various players react to different situations. This is what good players do. Some keep a notebook with them and make regular entries; others, including most experts, have long memories. In the future, this recollection will come in handy when you're again facing these same players.

For example, in an effort to keep the size of the pot down, a particular player might raise only twice the size of the big-blind with a speculative hand, such as a small pair or suited connectors. But in an effort to limit the field, he may raise to four times the big blind with bigger pairs or AK. Astute observation identifies tendencies such as this, allowing you to make an educated guess as to the strength of an opponent's hand.

Try to determine which players would be more likely to call an all-in bet by you. To make your judgments, note such factors as your opponents' aggressiveness, stack size, style of play, how often they make or call all-in bets, and the strength of the hands you get to see. You may observe that some players practically never lay down a hand once they're involved in a pot, while others may not call an all-in bet unless they have the nuts or close to it. Developing these observational skills will be helpful when you progress to the "Advanced Basic Strategy," where you use some judgment in your decision-making.

Also, practice keeping track of the size of the pot. This is an important skill to develop if your plan is to continue your advancement to include skilled post-flop play, where you add some subjective judgment to your decision making by calculating "pot odds" (see "Counting Outs," pg. 130).

VARIATIONS TO BASIC STRATEGY

The basic strategy is, by necessity, very simple. But over-simplification of this complex game leaves some holes that can be exploited by observant opponents. These weaknesses are outlined and addressed in depth in the "Basic Plus" and "Expert" sections of this book. As a transition, here are some variations to KP Basic that fall on the cusp between Basic and Basic Plus. Integrating these moves into your game will make it much more powerful and unpredictable, perhaps allowing you to trap opponents into making costly mistakes. These variations need not be learned before employing the basic strategy. They can be added one at a time as you gain proficiency and confidence.

1. If the only time you raise less than all-in pre-flop is with AA or KK, players will adjust accordingly. One way to keep them guessing is to occasionally make an AA-type raise with lesser hands. Not only does this expand the number of hands you can play, thereby allowing you to pick up blinds that help maintain your stack size, it also occasionally traps an opponent into misreading the strength of your hand.

From any position, deviate from the basic strategy (slightly more than) 25% of the time with Group 2 hands by raising about one-sixth of your stack. One way to randomize this play is to make it whenever you have a red AK or a pair of queens of the same color. If re-raised, move in with Group 1 hands, but fold Group 2. If called pre-flop, move in on the flop with AA, or if your pair is an overpair to the cards on the board, such as QQ with a flop of J-9-2, or if your hand is AK and an ace or king flops. If one or more overcards flop when you have kings or queens, you aren't necessarily beaten, but you must proceed cautiously. The reason for this is that a likely holding an opponent will call with, but not re-raise with pre-flop, is AK. In this situation, you need to find out where you are in the hand. If your opponent is first to act and bets, you should fold. If you're first to act or your opponent checks to you, a bet of about 75%-100% of the pot should help define your situation. If your opponent raises or calls and bets on a subsequent betting round, you should fold unless you make a set. You should, however, be aware of the possibility that an opponent could call your bet on the flop with a draw and bluff on a later round.

2. In late position, you can occasionally attempt to pick up the blinds by raising five-to-seven times the big blind with Group 1-4 hands. With Group 1-3 hands, apply the above post-flop strategy if you're called pre-flop. With Group 4, move in if you flop a set. Or, with AQs, move in if you make a pair of queens, two pair, a flush, or have a flush draw. Otherwise take a free card if it's checked to you and hope to check it down if you don't improve. If your opponent bets, fold.

3. Effective play in the blinds is essential for tournament success (at least one-fifth of the hands you look at are from one of the blind positions). Be aware that players sometimes limp in early position with AA or KK, hoping to get raised so they can re-raise. Taking a flop is often an effective strategy. This gives you the potential to flop a monster and trap the trapper for all his money. Be more likely to call from the small blind or check from the big blind, rather than raise, with Groups 3-10 when there are early-position limpers. With Groups 1-2, move in.

4. When in the small blind, basic strategy calls for either raising or folding. Here are some other options for small-blind play.

• In an unraised pot early in a tournament, frequently calling, rather than folding or moving in, gives you a chance to flop a big hand and perhaps win a big pot. If you have a huge stack, calling with Group 2-6 hands, rather than folding, is an option. If you have a big stack, occasionally calling with Group 2-6, rather than moving in, is also a good way to mix things up.

• If you have a huge stack at later stages of a tournament when there are antes as well as blinds, you should expand the range of hands for the above strategy. Your tactic at this point should be to follow the basic strategy as far as moving in, but call the amount of the big blind, rather than fold, with hands up to and including Group 10.

The above strategies can also be used when you're on the button. The playing advantage of acting last on each post-flop betting round can make calling, rather than folding, a profitable tactic, even for a player with limited post-flop skills. Post-flop, follow the strategies provided for post-flop play in both the KP Basic and KP Plus sections, depending on your level of advancement.

Online Variations

The fact that we've loosened the basic strategy for online play eliminates the need for many variations. The variations that apply online involve play from the blinds and late stages—variations 3 and 4 above.

Additionally, in the later stages, online tournaments become more like live affairs. This is primarily due to the fact that most (but not all) of the weaker players have been eliminated. If you're versed in both the standard and online basic strategies, revert to the live-tournament game plan when you've made it into the money. This usually means that about 10% of the field remains. Final-table online play is the same as live play.

As players become more aware of the specifics of the Kill Phil strategy, some of the plays will become less effective, and more variations will be required to keep opponents guessing. We'll use our Web site, KillPhilPoker. com as a forum to keep our players ahead of the curve by developing more variations to the strategy based on how other players are adjusting.

Part Three

The Kill Phil
Intermediate
Strategies

8

KILL PHIL BASIC PLUS

In poker, ... you will earn or lose money in accordance
with the quality of your decisions.
—Mike Caro

The cornerstone of the Kill Phil strategy is the all-in move. The power of this move is what frustrates and confuses your more skilled opponents. At this point, our prototype Kill Phil player is not yet ready to get in there and slug it out with the small-ball wizards. The all-in game is still the core of the strategy, but now we'll begin to refine it to make it more powerful.

The KP Basic is a system that requires little thinking or judgment. It's a simple, yet effective, answer to a complex question. It's rare to find a gambling situation like this, but the nature of NLH tournaments makes it possible. It's a big jump from KP Basic to the type of game played by the great poker pros, but there are some steps you can take, without fully immersing yourself, that make the strategy more effective. Basic Plus requires you to use some judgment in the application of the strategy. As you move beyond Basic, you'll begin to think like a poker player. The most important areas that you'll be addressing are adjustments for and awareness of CSI, opponents' stack sizes, playing players, and table composition. Other areas to consider are avoiding traps, table image, and the pace of play at your table.

We use the terms "tighten" or "loosen" your hand requirements in some of the examples that follow. By tighten we mean to play fewer hands. If the strategy calls for making a play with Group 1-6, for example, you might want to temporarily eliminate Group 6, or possibly Groups 5 and 6.

When you tighten, it's because you think you have a better chance of being called. By eliminating your weaker hand groups, you increase the chances that, if called, you'll have the best hand. The first hands you should eliminate are the suited connectors of Group 6.

To loosen is to play more hand groups than called for in KP Basic. You'll generally be less likely to loosen than to tighten, but there are occasions when it's called for.

CSI ADJUSTMENTS

The CSI break points in KP Basic are designed to be easily calculable. However, there's a lot of leeway. Let's say the blinds are 100-200, with a 25 ante. Whether your stack is 2,300 or 5,300, the CSI puts you in the medium-stack category. But as you can see, there's a lot of room for interpretation. With 2,300, your strategy should lean more toward that for a short stack; with 5,300 you should lean more toward big-stack parameters.

PLAYING ACCORDING TO STACK SIZES

A very important factor in an opponent's decision on whether to play or fold when you've raised relates to stack sizes. In order to anticipate how your opponent might act, you should constantly monitor your opponents' stack sizes, as well as your own.

Let's break the situations down into when you're the original raiser or the re-raiser.

If you're the first raiser, an opponent is less likely to call in the following circumstances:

• If he has a small stack, but isn't desperate.
• If you and he both have similar-sized medium-to-big stacks.

Your opponent is more likely to call in the following instances:

• If he's in a desperate situation with a very small stack.
• If he has a big stack and you have a small stack.
• If he's in one of the blinds (big blind more likely to call than small blind) and you have a small stack.

If you re-raise, the original raiser is more likely to call:

• If he raised from early position.
• If his raise was a significant portion (more than a third) of his stack.
• If you have a much smaller stack than him.
• If you've re-raised frequently.

The original raiser is less likely to call a re-raise:

• If he raised from a late position.
• If you both have huge/big stacks.
• If you have a bigger stack than he does and you're close to the money.

• If he's a great player and would be eliminated if he calls and loses.

In all of the above examples, adjustments should be made toward tightening your play when your opponent is more likely to call and loosening your play when he's less likely to call.

PLAYING THE PLAYER

A poker axiom is that you play the player, not the cards. Understanding your opponents allows you to make judgments about the strength of their holdings and predict their actions. The way you get to know your opponent is through observation. Pay close attention to the hands of your opponents that you get to see. The following are things you want to know.

Is He Experienced or Inexperienced?

Name players and experienced players are more likely to back down to an all-in raise or re-raise than inexperienced players, who are more unpredictable. Experienced players generally look for situations where they're huge favorites. This is seldom the case pre-flop. Their strategy is to see a lot of flops and steal a lot of blinds. Your strategy of all-in raises and re-raises foils their game plan.

Many of the players that you encounter in major tournaments around the world won their entries in online satellites. If players unfamiliar to you are wearing clothing with a logo from an online poker site, you can be pretty sure they got in this way. Don't be hesitant to ask questions to determine their level of experience. Most newer players are more than happy to find a friendly face (for a laugh, if you're ever seated with Phil Hellmuth, ask him if it's his first tournament).

Inexperienced players need to be carefully observed. Try to determine if they're timid, aggressive, or act irrationally. Against timid players, tend to loosen your raising requirements, especially in the later stages of a tournament. This is the time to be the bully. However, you must tighten your re-raising standards. If a timid player enters a pot with a raise, especially if it's from early position, you can be fairly sure he has a strong hand.

Against inexperienced aggressive players, tend to tighten your re-raising standards, because they'll likely call your re-raise with weaker hands than you'd expect. Likewise, players who act unpredictably require caution. Tend to tighten against them too.

Is He Tight or Loose?

It's important to notice what percentage of pots a player enters and how he responds to raises and re-raises, adjusting your strategy accordingly. Making written notes when playing online is a sound tactic. (We know one online player who has a dossier on all the online opponents he's encountered. He maintains a ledger book with detailed entries on the tendencies and styles of the competition. He's played so many hours in online tournaments that he'll usually have encountered more than half the players at his table. He's won a lot of money, so his diligence has been rewarded.)

A tight player will have strict requirements for raising and usually won't get involved in pots raised by others players without a premium hand. If a tight player on your right has raised, dramatically tighten your re-raising requirements. With tight players to your left, however, you should steal more frequently, because they'll play only the strongest of hands. In this situation, steal attempts with less than all-in raises are an effective tool (however, if you get played with, proceed cautiously).

Weak-tight players are passive and predictable. When they raise, they generally have a strong hand and you should proceed cautiously. When they limp, though, they'll almost always surrender to a significant raise. You should play against them accordingly.

There are different types of loose players. Some of the top pros, like Phil Hellmuth, Phil Ivey, and Daniel Negreanu, play a lot of hands pre-flop and rely on their ability to outplay their opponents post-flop. These guys are Phils. Your strategy is to avoid playing with them post-flop, where they have a significant advantage. However, they're generally reluctant to call an all-in bet pre-flop without a big hand. Loosen your requirements a bit and pound on them with your all-in pre-flop moves.

Less skilled players may also be involved in a lot of hands, but they don't possess the talent to play effectively post-flop. Unlike the Phils, they also have a tendency to call frequently, even all-in bets. This type of player is referred to as a "calling station." You never want to bluff a calling station. Against these players, you should tighten your requirements. Your strategy is to play strong hands, hoping to get called by weaker ones.

Is He a Bully?

In poker, bullies win. Watch any good player and you'll see someone who tries to dominate the table. Some players, such as Sammy Farha, will get you down and never let you up, especially when he has lots of chips. Paul Phillips is a nice gentle guy away from the table, but at the table his goal is to slap you around like he's Mike Tyson in a bad mood. He has bad intentions for your chips. Players like this use their chips as weapons. They want to beat you into submission as they watch your stack dwindle into insignificance. To combat bullies, you must fight back. Bullies don't like being hit. If they get hit a few times, they withdraw in favor of picking on softer targets. Why should they risk getting hurt tangling with you when they can easily fatten up their stacks by intimidating timid patsies? But if you let them, they'll continue to brazenly bash you around, too. You mustn't let them. Fight back aggressively. Don't let them become the dominator. One of the idiosyncrasies of the Kill Phil strategy is that it often does better at a table populated by good, rather than mediocre, players. That's because good players more readily fold when re-raised than less-skilled players. Re-raising is a powerful weapon against the Phils.

As a Basic Plus player, your analysis of the above factors is directed toward answering one pivotal question: What kind of hand does your opponent need in order to call your raise or re-raise? The more likely he seems willing to race, the more you should tighten your requirements. Conversely, the tighter he plays, the more you should loosen up, unless you both have huge stacks.

To illustrate this point, if all players have stack sizes of 30X the blinds, and you know for sure that all players will call your all-in bet only with AA, it's correct to raise with the top 89% of hands, even from first position! However, if we change the hands the other players will call with to both AA and KK, now it's correct to move in only with AA or KK from first position.

Given two players with stack sizes of 30X the blinds (small blind versus big blind), if the big blind calls your all-in bet only with AA, KK, QQ, JJ, and AK suited, it's correct to move in with *any* two cards!

As you can see, the correct raising strategy is highly sensitive to the number of hands opponents will call with.

THE POWER OF THE RE-RAISE

In *Tournament Poker for Advanced Players,* David Sklansky presents an idea he calls the "gap concept." His theory is that in NLH, you need a far better hand to call a raise than you need to raise with. We concur. However, in his *System*, Sklansky limits his re-raising strategy to only the strongest hands. We think the re-raise has wider applicability. Here's why.

While the all-in move is great for the all-important task of picking up blinds and antes, the real power of the Kill Phil strategy is the re-raise. Most players are hesitant to raise from the early positions without a good hand. This makes sense, because a number of players still have to act and they could pick up a big hand. In unopened pots, players lower their raising standards as their position improves. A good aggressive player in the cutoff or button position often makes a play at the pot with almost any hand.

KP Basic is designed to consider these factors. Re-raising requirements are strict against early-position raisers. They become more liberal as we consider middle-position raisers. Against players in the steal positions, we advocate an aggressive re-raising stance.

Many players make late-position raises with marginal hands that must be folded to a re-raise. A number of young Scandinavian players have recognized this and are employing this counter-strategy in the extreme. When Lee played in a recent tournament in the Caribbean, one of the Scandinavian players made an all-in re-raise almost every time Lee raised from the cutoff or the button. Lee was put in the position of not being able to steal pots from late position. Without that ploy in his arsenal, his overall edge in the tournament was greatly reduced.

The Kill Phil system is a bit more refined than the Scandinavians'. By re-raising nearly every time, the Scandinavian player forced Lee to limp more, rather than attempt to steal the pot with a raise. Although this allowed Lee to see a lot of flops with the advantage of position, the goal of the Kill Phil strategy is to avoid post-flop play. By the KP players re-raising all-in only a reasonable percentage of the time, late-position players are discouraged from trying to steal too often, but they'll still take stabs at some pots. Then, with a qualifying hand, our re-raise, if uncalled, will garner the blinds, antes, and the amount of the raise, making up for the chips we might have won had we gotten a free flop. If called, our hand usually has a reasonable chance of prevailing, if it's not already the best hand.

While writing this book, we noticed how often our normal small-ball tournament strategy put us in a position where we'd raised, but couldn't call a re-raise. Fortunately, most of the time, the other players passed. But when they did re-raise, we'd usually be forced to muck. Let's look at an actual example from a large online tournament involving an excellent player.

With 100 players left from a starting field of 1,200, the blinds were 1,500-3,000 with a 200 ante. Crocodile Bill Argyros, a top Australian player, had 36,000. It was passed around to him in the cutoff position. He raised to 9,000 with AQ off-suit. The button, with 52,000 in chips, moved in. Billy had several things to consider: What hands could the re-raiser have, what type of player is he, could he be bluffing, is it correct mathematically to call based on pot odds, etc. He was in a quandary. When faced with a tough call, this is the type of thought process that goes into the ultimate decision-making. Billy, thinking like a good player, backed down and never found out if his laydown was correct. Such is the power of the re-raise. (Note that this is exactly the kind of dilemma the Kill Phil strategy avoids. The KP strategy recommends an all-in bet in this situation with Billy's hand.)

Adjusting to different playing styles is essential to tournament success. By using constant observation, you'll discover the tendencies of your adversaries. Be they timid mice or pugnacious bullies, you'll have an answer for their moves. Be aware that as the blinds and antes increase, your opponents may change their approach, generally becoming more aggressive.

TABLE COMPOSITION

Most of the adjustments you should make against specific players were covered in "Playing the Player," pg. 106. However, you should be aware that the overall nature of play at your table, known as "table pace," can change radically depending on the line-up of players. Over the course of a tournament, this changes repeatedly as players are eliminated and replaced. Sometimes your table will be closed and you'll be faced with an entire new line-up. At other times a single player can dramatically change the pace of your table. Here's an example.

At a WPT tournament at the Bicycle Club in Los Angeles, Blair was cruising along nicely at a table consisting of mostly timid non-threatening players. He'd increased his stack from 5,000 to about 9,000 and was feeling in control. A lady directly to his left was playing very timidly, nursing a small stack. This is the kind of player you want to have on your left, and Blair was rooting for her to hang in there for a while. Unfortunately, she got knocked out. And who should come to replace her? None other than Gus Hansen, one of the most notorious of the Phils, with a stack bigger than Blair's. Over the next three hours, Gus either called or raised virtually every pot that wasn't raised in front of him, and many that were. He picked up a lot of pots un-contested and got lucky in some others. Suddenly, he had a monstrous stack. Every time it was passed to Blair in the small blind, if he called, Gus raised. Every time! Blair was handcuffed. He got few playable hands and was getting called or raised by Gus each time he entered a pot. If a different player had taken that seat, Blair probably would have been able to maintain his stack through aggressive play, while waiting to pick up a big hand. But with Gus in that position, his only option was to fight the bully. Blair decided that the next time he had a decent hand, he'd play back at Gus. He picked up AK suited in the small blind and hoped that everyone would pass, which they did. Blair just called, Gus raised as expected, and Blair moved in. Blair had been prepared to loosen his hand requirements and challenge Gus with a much lesser hand, so the suited AK seemed providential. Finally, Gus was trapped. Blair was delighted when Gus called his all-in raise, thinking this was an excellent opportunity to both double-up and send a message to Gus that he couldn't be pushed around. Confidently, Blair rolled over his strong hand. Gus smiled, shook his head, and showed pocket aces! The best laid plans of mice and men …

TABLE IMAGE AND CHANGING GEARS

"Table image" is the perception other players have of a particular player. It's a collage composed of many factors. Taken together, these traits create an impression that influences how other players react to him. Mechanical factors include how many hands are played, how often pots are raised or re-raised, and what hands are shown down. Non-verbal indicators include physical aura or presence, how he bets his chips, his facial expressions, body language, and a host of other signals. Verbal messages round out the picture. Although you may think of poker players as stone-faced, many of the best players talk frequently, not only to help create an impression, but also to help get a read on the competition.

Throughout a tournament, players will be closely observing you. As per the strategy in KP Basic, at the early limits of a tournament you'll play extremely tight. In major tournaments, you may not play a hand for hours. Players notice this. If you're new to live tournaments, experienced players will realize that you're a newbie, and since you're playing so few hands, they'll assume that you're timid. As the limits increase, you'll become more active, and begin to implement your all-in strategy. Until you reach a point where you've been active in a number of pots or shown down a medium-strength hand, your opponents will retain that super-tight image of you. While they have this image, you can become a bit more liberal with your hand selection against opponents who you read as tight, or unwilling to gamble. You could even reinforce this move by saying something like, "Wow, I'm really picking up a lot of hands." If your opponents fear the strength of your hands, you can keep collecting those all-important blinds and antes.

Throughout a tournament, your table image will change. Try to see yourself as others see you. You need to make regular adjustments as you go along. This is called "changing gears." If you've been involved in some recent pots, tighten up. If you move in and show down a hand like suited connectors, your opponents will definitely notice and will tend to think that you've been moving in with less than premium hands. They'll be much more willing to call, so tighten your requirements. If you're very lucky, you'll pick up a big hand and trap an opponent who reads you as weak.

If you haven't been getting hands to play, consider loosening up a bit. Your opponents probably will interpret a protracted period of inactivity as a sign of tight play and will be more likely to give you credit for a strong hand. Repeatedly varying your play based on your recent history garners benefits throughout the tournament.

At later stages of a tournament, the image a KP player projects is one of a player who's subject to move in at any time and doesn't fear big confrontations. This is an image that keeps your opponents back-pedaling and fearful, knowing that all of their chips could be in jeopardy at any moment.

Kill Phil players become targets for the other players. That's good! When players are reacting to you, you have them off kilter. They'll be lying in wait for a big hand to bust you with. Proper changing of gears makes you an elusive target. A feel for tournament play, coupled with focused observation of your opponents and an understanding of how your play affects them, provides you with clues as to when to gear up and when to gear down.

THE MOVE-IN STAGE

At the latter stages of a tournament, the blinds and antes start to put a lot of pressure on the smaller stacks. When about ⅔ of the field has been eliminated, most tables will have several players with small-to-medium stacks. We refer to this as the move-in stage.

The move-in stage is long-ball territory. Players frequently go all-in pre-flop, often with marginal hands. As a rule, the first one in takes the pot, as opponents with similar stacks are loathe to call with medium-strength hands when their tournament life is on the line. When you're the first to move in, you have two ways to win the pot—when your opponents fold or if your hand wins in a showdown. When you call another player's all-in move, you must win a showdown. With a medium-to-short stack, if you have a lukewarm holding, it's often better to wait for an opportunity where you can be the raiser, rather than the caller, unless you're desperate or conditions discussed later in this section dictate a call. With a big stack, however, your aim is to selectively pick off your desperate foes and send them packing.

Because players are moving in more frequently, a smaller percentage of pots are unopened by the time the action gets to you. Unless you have the security of a huge or big stack, you need to loosen your requirements when you have the chance to be first in, in order to keep from getting eaten alive by the blinds and antes. If you pick up a big hand quickly and double up, that's great, but it's absolutely critical during this stage that you preserve a stack substantially large enough to pose a significant threat to most of the other competitors. Your goal is to tread water until a big hand comes along. If you allow your stack size to be blinded down to the point where other players have an easy call when you finally do move in, you've lost a huge amount of leverage. Rather than letting this occur, we'd prefer to move in with many hands that we'd never consider playing under less adverse circumstances. Given reasonably tight opponents, we'd consider moving in with any two cards from the button or the blinds in unraised pots, especially if there aren't any limpers.

> **Key Point:** It's essential to preserve your stack size so that it poses a significant threat to your opponents, even if it means taking greater risks than normal, such as moving in with any two cards from the button or the blinds in unraised pots with no limpers.

Here are our recommended modifications for the move-in stage:

Huge or Big Stack
Stick pretty close to KP Basic, but be on the lookout for opportunities to call all-in bets from desperate short stacks, especially when they're under the gun and the blinds are about to cripple them. Late-position all-in moves from desperate players are also suspect. Hands such as A8 or higher, or any pair, become calling hands, provided you're one of the last players to act and losing a race won't severely affect your stack size.

Medium Stack
Early Position:	Move in with Groups 1-6
Middle Position:	Move in with Groups 1-7

Cutoff: Move in with Groups 1-9
Button and either blind: Move in with Groups 1-10

If the blinds are tight players, consider moving in from the button or either blind with all but the weakest hands such as 32, 42, 52, 62, 72, 82, 43, 53, 63, 73, 83, 92, 93 and 32 suited, if there are no limpers.

Short Stack

Early position: Move in with Groups 1-8
Middle position: Move in with Groups 1-10
Cutoff, button, and either blind:
                          Consider moving in with any two cards if there are no limpers

Say you have 7,000 and the blinds are 600/1,200 with a 100 ante. Average chips are 20,000. It's costing you 2,800 per round, which is more than 1/3 of your stack. Most pots are being raised before the action gets to you. Finally, it's passed around to you in the cutoff. You have 8♦4♦, an unplayable hand under most circumstances. You check the stack sizes of the three players on your left. The button has 22,000, SB has 17,000, and BB has 10,000. From what you've observed, their calling requirements for an all-in bet are reasonably conservative. You're aware that if you don't find a hand to play until after the blinds come around, you'll have about 4,500 left—less than twice the blinds and antes and a totally unthreatening stack—so you decide to move in now. Although 8♦4♦ isn't a basic-strategy-recommended hand to play, during the move-in stage under circumstances like this, it makes sense. Here's why.

Your all-in bet is big enough to cripple or damage the

remaining players, none of whom can comfortably afford to lose 7,000. They probably won't call without a big-ace (AT or better) or a reasonable pair (66 or better). There's about a 90% chance that your opponents will fold to your all-in bet. This means you'll add a much needed 2,800 to your stack about 90% of the time. The other 10% of the time you'll have to race for all your chips, and you'll undoubtedly be behind. With a hand like 8♦4♦, your cards are unlikely to be duplicated, except in rare occasions, such as by 88. You may feel pretty foolish when the BB calls and shows you AK and you're forced to expose your paltry 84 suited, but how big an underdog are you? You'll still win just over 38% of the time. Not great, but you're far from a cinch to lose. Should you win, you'll suddenly have 16,500, nearly average chips. Even if your opponent has two black aces, you'll still win roughly 19% of the time—pretty bad, but still, not necessarily fatal.

Adjusting your play in this manner during the move-in stage is essential for maintaining your chip stack during this critical phase. As usual, judgment is required. Big stacks, maniacs, and calling stations on your left are more likely to call your all-in gambit. In these instances, you may need to tighten up a bit, but don't overdo it.

Preserving your chip stack provides the firepower to stay aggressive. If they take you out, it won't be with a whimper.

Calling Raises During the Move-In Stage

Due to the fact that players are moving in with more hands than usual, you may be inclined to call with more hands than you'd normally play. Lee was short-stacked, with 7,300 in the small blind, in an online tournament. The blinds were 600/1,200 with a 75 ante. It was passed around to an aggressive player on the button, who moved in for more than 50,000. Lee had A4 off-suit. The big blind was also short-stacked with 10,000. Lee reasoned that in this situation, the raiser would move in with a lot of hands, many of which he could beat. Lee decided to call and race. If he won, he'd have close to average chips. If he lost, he'd be out. As it happened, his opponent had A5 off-suit, but a board of 2-2-K-3-8 resulted in a split pot.

A little later, Lee, now with 10,500, mucked the same hand—A4 off-suit in early position. He wasn't quite as desperate at that point and didn't need to get involved with a marginal hand with six players yet to act behind him. However, had it been passed to him in the cutoff, button, or small blind with this same hand, he would have moved in. Judgment calls such as this are common during this phase of a tournament and can make a big difference as to whether or not you make it to the final table. When in doubt, stay aggressive!

Rounding Up the Desperados

Desperate players do desperate things. One of the most common moves they make is moving in under the gun when the blinds will decimate their remaining stack on the next hand. Because first-position bets are generally interpreted as representing strength, they'd often prefer to make this move, hoping to pick up the blinds, as opposed to waiting until the next hand when someone will surely put them all-in. Knowing that players in this spot can have virtually anything, you can substantially loosen your calling requirements when you have a medium-to-large stack. Lee recently called an all-in under-the-gun desperado raise with A7 in the 6-seat, after the other players before him had passed. The raiser had J7 off-suit and was knocked out.

Desperados also tend to become active in unopened pots when they're in late position or in the blinds. In a big tournament in Melbourne, Lee was the chip leader. In a small blind-big blind confrontation, a solid aggressive young player in desperation mode moved in on Lee, who called with jack high. His shocked opponent meekly turned over 10 high! Lee's jack held up and the desperado hit the trail. Under normal circumstances, neither player would have played this way. But desperate times call for desperate measures, and countermeasures.

Modifying Your Play Based on Table Image

During the move-in stage, be careful not to overdo the all-in move. If you've been uninvolved for a while, you can loosen your move-in requirements, but if you've successfully moved in a couple of times, tighten your standards. The more often your opponents see you making this move, the more likely they are to call. This is when it's great to wake up with a big hand. After you've moved in a few times, your disbelieving foes are subject to call. When they do, it's pretty sweet if you can show them a big pair. Stay aware as to how active you've been and adjust your involvement accordingly.

9

FINE-TUNING KILL PHIL BASIC PLUS

Seldom do the lambs slaughter the butcher.
—Amarillo Slim

ADVANCED POST-FLOP STRATEGY

One way to carry the KP philosophy into post-flop play is to keep putting pressure on your opponents. The all-in strategy works post-flop in a similar way to pre-flop. Players put to a decision for all or most of their stack by an all-in bet generally need a very strong hand to call.

Many post-flop hand match-ups are close to a coin flip. However, the threat of the all-in player having flopped a monster often forces a player to fold a hand he'd play if he knew his opponent's cards. Following are some examples.

You	Opponent	Flop
K♥Q♥	Q♠J♠	3♥-4♥-J♣

Your opponent is an 11-10 favorite; it's a near coin flip. However, if you move in, he must fear that you already have him beat with a hand like a set, two pair, an overpair, or a jack with a better kicker. His hand is not very strong. You'd like him to fold, which he most likely will. But if he calls, you'll still win almost half the time. The extra chips already in the pot make your play mathematically correct, and it's even more correct when you're up against a Phil, who's even more likely to fold such a hand.

You	Opponent	Flop
8♥9♥	Q♠J♠	3♥-4♥-J♣

In this example, your opponent is slightly more than an 8-5 favorite; it's not a situation you really want to race with. This situation calls for a check and fold if your opponent bets. We don't recommend moving in every time you have a draw. If you mix up your play, your opponents have a hard time putting you on a hand.

You	Opponent	Flop
6♥5♥	A♠A♣	3♥-4♥-J♣

This time, even though your opponent has aces and you don't have a pair yet, you're a 13-10 favorite! This is a case where your opponent will likely call and have the worst of it. Appendix VI has more examples of post-flop match-ups.

THE STRATEGY

Once you've reached this point, your experience and observation in real-time tournament situations should have helped you to develop a feel for small-ball-style post-flop play. While we don't focus on small-ball techniques in this book, as a Basic Plus player you'll find yourself involved a bit more post-flop, so we've included some guidelines for a more advanced post-flop strategy. Remember, it's impossible to cover all the situations that can arise, so use your best judgment when applying these strategies. Your goal is to mix up your play, keep your opponents off-balance, and hopefully trap them when you flop a big hand.

Important considerations in post-flop strategy are pot size, position, number of opponents in the pot, your stack size, and the size of your opponents' stacks. We break the strategy down into the following situations:

1. Heads up, unraised pot, and you act first.
2. Heads up, unraised pot, and you act last.
3. Multi-way pot.
4. Raised pot.

Heads-Up, Unraised Pot, You Act First

If you flop 4-of-a-kind, a straight flush, a full house, a flush, a straight, a set, 3-of-a-kind, or 2-pair with an unpaired board (hereafter referred to as a Group 1 flop), you've flopped a big hand. In order to maximize your chances of winning a big pot with your powerhouse, mix it up between the following three options:

• Move in.
• Bet 50% of your chips on the flop. If called, move in on the turn.

- Check-raise all-in on the flop.

With quads, a straight flush, or a full house you should definitely check the flop. If your opponent bets, just call and see what he does on the turn. Your goal is to get him to put all his chips in at some point. With a less powerful hand, the more vulnerable your hand is, the more likely you should bet half your chips or move in on the flop. The more connected the board with straight or flush possibilities, the less you want to risk giving a free card by attempting a check-raise. With a 3-straight or 3-flush on the board, giving a free card is risky business—move in. While it's possible that your opponent already has a made straight or flush and you'll be jumping right into the mouth of the lion, even in this case you'll usually have outs. It's a risk you'll have to take.

If you attempt a check-raise gambit and your opponent fails to oblige by betting after you've checked, you'll have to make another decision on the turn. If the turn card doesn't appear to put your hand in jeopardy, bet half or all of your chips. If the card is a bad one for your hand, you should proceed cautiously. For example, if you flopped a small flush and the turn is a fourth card of your suit, you should check and fold to any action.

If, with an unpaired board, you flop top pair with an ace-kicker or an overpair:
- With a small or medium stack, move in.
- With a huge/big stack, if your opponent has a small or medium stack, move in.
- If you both have huge/big stacks and there's no 2- or 3-straights or flushes on the board, check-raise all-in 50% of the time; otherwise, bet the size of the pot and, if raised, move in. Move in on the turn no matter what happens. The bigger the pot, the more likely you should be to bet,

rather than attempt a check-raise.

• If you both have huge/big stacks and there's a 3-straight or flush on the board, move in on the flop unless the pot is very small relative to your stack size, in which case, check and fold to a bet.

Note: If there's a pair on board, bet/raise all-in with 3-of-a-kind/top kicker or better.

If, with an unpaired board, you flop top pair without an ace-kicker:

• With a small or medium stack, move in.

• With a huge/big stack, move in if your opponent has a small-to-medium stack.

• If both you and your opponent have huge/big stacks, proceed with caution. Either try to just check it down or make a bet of around 75% of the pot size. If called, try to check it down, but fold if your opponent makes a significant bet.

Note: If there's a pair on board, bet/raise all-in with 3-of-a-kind/top kicker or better.

Heads-Up, Unraised Pot, You Act Last

With a Group 1 flop:

• If your opponent bets, vary your play between moving in and smooth-calling. The more vulnerable your hand, the more you should consider moving in. For example, if you have 98 of spades and the flop is 9-8-7 with two hearts, even though you have top 2-pair, your hand is in jeopardy. Make it expensive for your opponent to draw to his hand—move in. This also avoids the possibility of having to make a difficult decision on the turn if a "scare card" comes and he bets again. Other vulnerable hands include bottom 2-pair, small straights, and small flushes.

• If your opponent checks, bet 3-5 times the size of the pot. If he raises, move in. If he calls, move in on the turn.

If, with an unpaired board, you flop top pair with an ace-kicker or an overpair:
• If your opponent bets, move in regardless of your stack size.
• If it's checked to you, move in with a small or medium stack or if you have a huge/big stack and your opponent has a small-to-medium stack.
If you both have huge/big stacks, bet 3-5 times the size of the pot. The more connected the flop, the more you should bet. If check-raised, your hand is probably second-best. Folding is your best option.
Note: If there's a pair on board, bet/raise all-in with 3-of-a-kind/top kicker or better.

If, with an unpaired board, you flop top pair without an ace-kicker:
• If your opponent bets, move in with a small-to-medium stack or with a huge/big stack if your opponent has a small stack.
If you have a huge/big stack and your opponent has a medium stack, you have a tough decision. Your tendency should be toward preserving your stack. Unless you have a good reason to get involved—such as your opponent makes a small bet, or you have a straight or flush draw along with your pair, or you have a good read on your opponent as being weak—you should fold.
If you both have huge/big stacks, fold.
• If your opponent checks, move in with a small or medium stack or if you have a huge/big stack and your opponent has a small-to-medium stack.
If you both have huge/big stacks, bet 3-5 times the size of

the pot. The more connected the flop, the more you should bet. If check-raised, your hand is probably second-best. Folding is your best option. If called, proceed with caution.

Note: If there's a pair on board, bet/raise all-in with 3-of-a-kind/top kicker or better.

Multi-Way Unraised Pot

Play the same way as in "Basic Post-Flop Play" (pg. 83), with the exception that if you flop a set in an unconnected flop, you may want to go for an all-in check-raise.

Raised Pot

Basic Plus players occasionally find themselves in the position of seeing a flop in a raised pot. The strategy in this case is the same as outlined above, with the additional tactics discussed in "Variations to Basic Strategy" #1 and #2 (pgs. 96-97).

If You Flop a Draw

What you do should be based on three factors:

The size of the pot—The bigger the pot, the more you should be willing to risk to try to win it.

Your stack size and that of your opponents—Be especially wary about moving in with a draw when you have a big or huge stack and you're up against one or more opponents who also have huge/big stacks. In situations such as this, it's best to try to make your hand cheaply, while preserving your imposing stack size. If you make your hand on the turn or river, you can win a big pot without having seriously jeopardized your chips without a made hand.

The quality of your draw—Occasionally, you'll have a

draw that's so strong, you'd welcome a call, but in most cases you're hoping to win uncontested. If you limit the times you move in to only the strongest draws, you'll have the best chance if you get called. Some examples of good draws are listed here:

Your Hand	Flop	Draw
J♣T♦	T♥-9♣-8♦	Straight draw, open-ended with a pair
K♥Q♥	J♥-T♠-4♣	Straight draw, open-ended with 2 overcards
A♥9♥	9♣-7♥-2♥	Flush draw with pair
T♥9♥	8♥-6♥-4♣	Flush draw with a straight draw
K♥Q♥	8♥-4♥-2♣	Flush draw with 2 overcards

Note that you don't want to draw to a straight if there's a flush draw on board or draw to a flush if the board is paired. Finally, if there are two or three cards 9 or higher on the board, it's much more likely that an opponent has a hand he can call with.

COUNTING OUTS

You'll often hear poker players use the term "outs" when discussing hands. You might hear something like, "I had 12 outs on the flop, but didn't get there." Or, "He hit a 3-outer on me." Outs are cards that improve a hand from a loser to a winner.

With one card left to come, it's a simple math problem. For example, you're all-in with K♥Q♥ and the board reads J♠-T♣-2♥-3♦. Your opponent turns over J♣T♦. You'll win with any ace or nine. This gives you a total of 8 outs. You've seen 8 cards (yours and your opponent's, plus the four board cards), so there are 44 cards left unseen. Subtracting your 8 outs from the 44 unseen cards leaves 36 cards that are losers. Hence, your chances of winning are 36/8, or 4.5-1 against.

While it's nice to know your chances in a showdown situation, the real value in counting outs is to estimate the value of your hand when both you and your opponent have chips left and there are more cards to come. In the above example, say your opponent bet 2,000 into a 2,400 pot and you have 800 left. You're confident that you'll win the pot if you make your straight. The pot is laying you 4,400/800, or 5.5-1. Since you're only a 4.5-1 dog, you're getting the right price, or proper "pot odds," to call. If you had 2,000 left, you'd be getting 4,400/2000, or only 2.2-1, so you'd be incorrect to call.

When you count outs, you must be careful not to double-count straight and flush cards. Say you have 9♥8♥ and the board reads J♥-T♣-2♥. From the betting, you suspect that your opponent has either AJ or an overpair. You're confident you'll win if you make either the straight or the flush. There are nine unseen hearts (3♥, 4♥, 5♥, 6♥, 7♥, T♥, Q♥, K♥, and A♥), plus four queens and four sevens that will complete your straight. That's 17 cards. However, two of the straight cards are hearts (7♥, Q♥) that you've already counted, so you can't count them again. The six remaining straight cards give you a total of 15 outs, which makes you about a 6-5 favorite.

With two cards to come, 13 outs give you just under a 50% chance of winning a showdown and 14 outs make you a slight favorite. (See Appendix VIII for the odds of making your hand with one or two cards to come, depending on the number of outs.) Knowing these numbers is a valuable tool.

TRAPPING AND AVOIDING TRAPS

"Trapping" involves disguising the strength of your hand to lure other players into incorrectly reading you as being weak. If successful, an opponent may get over-aggressive with a weaker hand or bluff his chips off to you. Trapping is the most successful countermeasure against the super-aggressive players of today. It can be used both pre-flop and post-flop, depending on circumstances.

Pre-Flop Trapping

Let's say the button raises and you're fortunate enough to wake up with aces or kings in the big blind. Basic strategy calls for a re-raise of five to seven times the size of the raise and, if called, moving in on the flop regardless of what comes. This is sound play. But what if you sometimes smooth-call and check to your opponent on the flop? If he's an aggressive player, he'll likely bet. If you look uncertain, make a crying call, then once again check the turn, he'll likely bet again. This time it may be a bet big enough to blow you off the mediocre hand he thinks you have. Now you spring the trap and move in!

You may pick up considerably more chips playing a big hand this way than you would by initially re-raising and taking down a small pot. The problem with trapping is that the trapper can sometimes wind up getting caught in his own snare.

In the $1,500-buy-in no-limit hold 'em event at the 2003 WSOP with the blinds 25-50, a player in early position made it only 100 to go holding pocket queens. A player with AJ called and Blair, in the big blind, called the extra 50 with 63 off-suit. Why? He was getting over 5-1 on his 50 call and he had a chance to win a big pot if he flopped two pair, a set, or a straight. The flop was 4-5-7. Bingo! Blair checked, the queens bet, the AJ folded, and Blair called. When the dust settled, Blair had doubled up. The trapper had been well and truly trapped.

For advanced play, we recommend following these criteria in choosing when to trap pre-flop.

• Consider smooth-calling when a single good-sized raise hasn't been called prior to the action getting to you and you have AA, KK, or QQ. If there's been one or more callers after the raise, re-raise—don't try to trap. A big pair loses value in multi-way pots and is hard to fold after the flop.

• Randomize the times when you smooth-call. Re-raise about ⅔ of the time and smooth-call ⅓ of the time with a big pair. A good way to do this is to smooth-call whenever the pair is the same color. Mixed-color pairs occur twice as frequently as colored pairs, so this will automatically randomize your decisions.

• If you have an aggressive player on you left, consider trapping by just calling with a big pair in an unopened pot from the cutoff position onward. This play may be especially effective in small-blind/big-blind confrontations, where an aggressive opponent in the big blind often raises when the small blind just calls. When he raises, call and check the flop, giving him all the rope he needs to hang himself.

• Limping with a big hand is also an effective tactic when you have a bully seated on your left. Your call will usually be read as a sign of weakness. If he raises, just call and check it to him on the flop. Now when he bets, move in. Next time he won't be so eager to try to take the pot away from you.

Avoiding Pre-Flop Traps

Be suspicious of small bets that are out of character for aggressive players. Say a player who consistently raises to four times the big blind suddenly raises to only twice the big blind from late position. Red flags should immediately start waving. Why? Instead of trying to pick up the blinds as he usually does, he's made a weak bet that invites a call or re-raise. This type of play is often made to conceal a big hand. In this instance, be less likely to re-raise. Proceed with the idea of attempting to trap this trapper.

Another suspect play is when a player in one of the blinds calls a late-position raise and check-calls on the flop. If he checks again on the turn, it's probably best to check right behind him, unless your hand can stand to be check-raised. Be content to check again on the river if given the opportunity, if all you have is something like top pair. If he bets on the river, use your best judgment as to whether to call.

Trapping Post-Flop

Although with the KP strategy it won't occur very often, rare opportunities may arise to set post-flop traps. For example, you're in the big blind and an early-position limper is attempting to trap with pocket aces. You take a free flop with Q4 and the flop is Q-4-2. You check the flop and he bets. Everyone passes to you. You move in. He'll have a hard time laying down his aces and you're a 3-1 favorite!

Another instance could occur when it's passed around and the small blind calls. If you flop a monster in the big blind and the small blind bets, smooth-call. Move in on the turn, either as a bet or raise.

Avoiding Post-Flop Traps

Suppose you're in the big blind and it's passed around to the small blind, who just calls. You've got K4 offsuit. You check and see the flop, which comes K-8-2 rainbow. You've got top pair with a weak kicker. What to do? Your hand is too weak to move in, but too strong to check if it's checked to you. Considering the unconnected nature of this flop, the best course of action is to make a reasonable (pot-sized) bet, hoping to win it right there. If you get called, you should put on the brakes and check from this point on. If your opponent has a hand such as A8, he may be content to just check it down. We don't recommend standing any heat with this hand. If your opponent check-raises on the flop, or bets the turn, you should muck. Your opponent's call on the flop means he's probably got something he likes. Since no straight or flush draws are possible, he may have two pair, a set, or kings with a better kicker (perhaps KQ). You may have the best hand, but it's not a hand with which you want to contest a big pot. If you get any heat, pass and avoid the possible trap. Also remember, the more limpers there are, the more likely it is that someone's flopped a big hand. Beware!

PLAYING ACES

In KP Basic with aces or kings, we recommend making an initial raise sufficient to discourage calls from speculative hands (or a re-raise of five to seven times an initial raise) or simply moving in. More experienced players can benefit from mixing up their big-pair play, depending on the situation and the table composition. It's also noteworthy that while aces and kings are both extremely strong starting hands, aces are in a class of their own. Although hypothetical arcane scenarios can be imagined whereby prize-money considerations might warrant laying down pocket aces, for practical purposes, this possibility can be eliminated from consideration. Thinking about how to extract the most value from aces in different situations is a far more valuable pursuit. Considering we only pick up aces an average of once every 220 hands, the biggest problem is that we don't get them often enough.

Early in a Tournament

When the blinds are small, falling in love with aces can be a big mistake. If you allow new-school players to enter the pot cheaply, they can break you if they catch a flop. Making a large enough raise so that a call will be mathematically incorrect is one appropriate antidote.

Lee uses a similar tactic, especially early in online play. He'll make a substantial pre-flop raise with aces. This is the type of play many players make with medium pairs in an attempt to discourage callers. If re-raised, he'll mix up his play, sometimes moving in and sometimes smooth-calling. A smooth-call in this spot is consistent with a medium-pair holding. On the flop, he'll try for an all-in check-raise.

Making smaller raises with aces can open up a can of

worms. Here's an example of the kind of situations you can get into.

Say you're playing in the Big One—the World Series of Poker $10,000-buy-in main event—and after patiently waiting for almost two hours with the blinds at 50-100, you wake up with two black aces. Finally! You're in early position and don't want to lose your market, so you make it 200 to go, the minimum raise that doesn't reveal the strength of the monster you're holding. You get called by four other players. The flop is 6-9-T with two hearts. You're first to act and bet 900, about the size of the pot. The first three challengers fold, but after thinking for what seems an eternity, the last player calls. The next card is the deuce of hearts. What do you do with those aces now? The pot is 2,700 and you've got about 8,600 left. A pot-size bet and you're pretty much committed to play this hand to the end. If you check, you may be giving your opponent a free card to a drawing hand like JQ or a 4-flush. Worse still, *he* might make a pot-sized bet. Now you don't know if he has 2-pair, a set, a flush, a straight, or if he's interpreted your check as a sign of weakness and is betting a hand like top pair with a flush draw. Or perhaps he's on a complete bluff.

Suppose you take a different tack and bet 1,300 after the turn as a feeler bet and the other player raises 1,300. He seems to be baiting you to commit. At this point, you have to ask yourself if you're willing to put in the rest of your chips before you call that piddling 1,300 raise, because you can be pretty sure that he'll make an all-in bet if you check again on the river. If he's got the flush or straight, you're drawing dead. And if he has a set, you've got only two outs (about a 20-1 underdog). So his 1,300 raise is really a 7,300 commitment for you. Of course, he could be bluffing or semi-bluffing. The problem is you don't know where you're at in the hand and your opponent knows it.

Most players get married to those aces and just can't release them no matter how the betting goes. But if all the chips go in, you're most likely beat in this spot.

After the flop, top players think long and hard before getting totally committed with a big pair when multiple players have either limped in or called a small pre-flop raise. If they bet and are faced with an all-in raise, they'll often let it go unless they have a good read on their opponents. Less experienced players will often die with them, grumbling all the way to the airport on their way home after suffering the misfortune of having their aces cracked.

Playing Aces at Later Stages

Once the antes start, the percentage of pots that are raised increases dramatically, as players fight for the blinds and antes. The average stack now has a much lower CSI, which requires players to loosen up, and thus provides more opportunities for deceptive play with aces.

Limping with Aces

Up-front—Many players limp from early position, hoping to get raised so they can re-raise. We don't recommend this strategy for KP players, for whom limping in early position looks too suspicious. Limping often begets limping and aces don't play well post-flop in multi-way pots, so we think it's best to avoid this type of tricky situation. Simply move in and hope to get called.

Around back—Limping with aces around back in a pot where there are already several limpers can be a lucrative ploy, provided you have one or more very aggressive players yet to act on your left. Some players can't resist raising in this situation. By limping with your aces, you can set up a big play. If a player raises behind you, as anticipated, astute players up-front may call or even re-raise. Like you, they know this player can have anything and they may try to take the pot away right there with a re-raise. When it comes back around to you, move in. You'll either win a big pot straight away or, if called, be a big favorite to win a monster pot in a showdown.

One caveat—When you make this play, you need to be reasonably sure that a player on your left will raise. If you've noticed that the players to your left are the type who like to see cheap flops, it would be a mistake to play aces in this manner.

Varying the Size of Pre-Flop Raises

Varying the amount of your raises with aces can be deceptive. If other players have observed your standard huge raises with aces or kings, they may interpret a lesser raise as a sign of weakness.

One spot where a smaller-than-normal raise might be especially effective is in late position, when you have a medium-to-big stack. Say it's passed to you on the button and you've got aces. Instead of your normal big raise, you now raise three to four times the big blind. It may seem as though you're trying to pick up the blinds and antes cheaply. An aggressive player may read this as a sign of weakness and re-raise. Now you can confirm his incorrect read by smooth-calling. He's first to act post-flop and may well continue his effort to blast you out of the pot. Whether he bets or checks, move in.

Small raises with aces can set up cheap steal opportunities. Once other players have noticed this play with aces, you might consider making a similar raise with a good-sized stack in a similar late-position situation with any Group 1-

10 hand. Opponents, wary of your big stack and now fearful of aces, will likely lay down medium-strength hands.

The Most Deceptive Play of All

A lot of players understand the dynamics of the move-in stage and play accordingly. However, many players, even some of the best ones, fall into a pattern of moving in with medium-strength hands, but making smaller raises with big pairs, wanting to get them paid off. Astute players, knowing this, are more willing to call these all-in moves than one might think.

For example, in the 2005 final of the Ultimate Poker Challenge, Blair was down to the final three, along with Andy Bloch, who had over a million in chips, and Chau Giang, who had about 320,000. Blair had a little over 200,000. Chau was first to act on the button and moved in, putting 320,000 into a pot of 30,000; he'd been making similar moves throughout the final-table play. Andy made a very brave call with AJ. However, he'd correctly surmised that Chau didn't have a really big hand or he wouldn't have made that move. Chau sheepishly turned over KJ and was eliminated in third place (resulting in a nice bonus of almost $50K for Blair).

Part of the power of the Kill Phil strategy is that we move in with a range of hands all the way from low suited connectors to aces and kings. An occasional change-up from that strategy can be effective, but doing it too often lessens the effectiveness of your other all-in moves. Don't get too tricky, especially if you've been caught moving in with one of the weaker hands. Players will be gunning for you, and you could surprise someone. In situations such as this, moving all-in with aces may be interpreted as weakness and may be your most profitable option.

FOLDING KINGS

Proper observation and understanding of tournament situations and players can sometimes lead to unusual plays. Although it's very difficult to get away from kings before the flop, at times it's pretty clearly the right play. Both authors have done it in tournaments. While laying down kings pre-flop may seem like a spectacular play, when all factors involved are considered, the logic of doing so can become clear.

The first time the viewing public was exposed to this was in 1999 at the inaugural Tournament of Champions at the Orleans in Las Vegas. With six players remaining, David Chiu, the chip leader with 1.3 million, was dealt pocket kings. The pot was raised and David re-raised. Louis Asmo, known as a very tight player, paused briefly, then moved in for more than 600,000. The initial raiser passed. David went into the tank and finally showed his kings and mucked. Sheepishly, Louis showed David, and the shocked audience, his two aces. David, having preserved his big stack, went on to win the tournament.

Let's examine David's probable thought process. David had re-raised prior to the action getting to Louis. David knew that Louis had great respect for his play and was quite a conservative player, yet despite this, was willing to commit all his chips late in the tournament. David was the chip leader at this point and knew Louis wouldn't jeopardize his entire stack without an absolute monster. Given this situation, he probably reasoned that Louis had to have either aces or kings, so at best, he would be tied. But upon further analysis, it undoubtedly occurred to David that if Louis had kings, he'd probably want to make sure that an ace didn't flop prior to committing all his chips. This realization, combined with the significantly increased mathematical probability that Louis held aces (since David had two kings), was sufficient to convince David that Louis had aces.

Recently, in a 2004 WPT $10,000-buy-in (where each player started with 20,000 in chips) event at Bellagio, this hand came up.

A nervous player, who'd scarcely played a hand for over two hours and had about 18,000, limped in under the gun with blinds of 100-200. Blair, seated directly to his left with 27,000 and holding KK, raised to 700. It was passed to a player in the 7-seat, a well-known high-limit player who came over the top, making it 2,700 to go. To Blair's surprise, the tight player in first position now made it 6,000. Blair thought it through and came to the conclusion that the worst hand the tight player could have was kings, but he most likely had aces. Blair had only 700 invested, had to call an additional 5,300 with an active player behind him, and was reasonably certain the guy in the first seat would put him to a decision for a big bet on the flop. Discretion seemed the better part of valor and Blair folded. Sure enough, the flop contained three babies and the under-the-gun player bet 12,000.

We're not advocating that KP players lay down kings—play them as recommended in the strategy. The purpose of this section is to show you the thought process that experienced players use, so you can begin to think like a poker player.

CLOSE TO THE MONEY

When only one or two additional players need to be eliminated for the field to make it into the money, play often changes. Players with small stacks may try to survive by going into a shell and declining to play all but the very best hands. Good players with big stacks often become super-aggressive, taking advantage of the reluctance of other players to get involved.

With an average stack or greater, there's no reason to deviate from normal strategy. With a short stack, you need to ask yourself what's important to you. Are you content with getting a payday, but leaving yourself so short-stacked that making the final table is extremely unlikely? Or would you rather risk getting knocked out on the bubble for a much greater shot at the big money? Even pros have differing philosophies about this. Some prefer to make the money, and then gamble. Others set their sights on the final table. John Juanda has said that there's only one prize—first place.

This decision has practical significance. With a short stack, if your plan is to just squeak into the money, tighten your hand requirements. But if your intention is to go for the gold, this is a good time to play back at an aggressive opponent who may be overplaying a weak hand. In the main event of the Aussie Millions poker tournament a few years ago, Lee was down to two tables and close to the money. He was short-stacked and moved in with pocket 6s. He could have probably survived by passing this hand, but he had bigger goals in mind. As luck would have it, he wound up making quad 6s and doubled up. On the very next hand, he picked up pocket kings, doubled up again, and was off and running. Lee continued his aggressive play and, by the time it got down to the final table, he was the chip leader. This is a good example of how, if the lure of merely making the money is disregarded, a small stack can sometimes be parlayed into a big payoff.

Another opportunity at this juncture, when you have

a medium-to-big stack against aggressive competitors, is to re-raise one of the aggressive players. It's unlikely that he has a hand he can call your all-in move with. Phil Hellmuth says that he once raised 12 consecutive pots when close to the money without a challenge. This is unlikely in the modern poker climate. Players today are much more willing to fight the bully. Join the club.

PLAYING AGAINST A MANIAC

Maniacs are very reckless players. They play a lot of pots and are quite unpredictable. While this sounds a lot like some of the good new-school players, the new-schoolers have a method to their madness, while the maniacs have little logic behind their play. They are, after all, maniacs. If you have a player like this at your table, you need to tighten a bit. He's much more likely to call your all-in bet or raise, so you want to have a good hand before getting involved with him. Suited connectors lose power against this type of opponent. However, a maniac is more susceptible to being trapped than a thinking player, so you should be more likely to employ the trapping strategies if you get involved with him.

RUSHES

A "rush" is when a player has a series of winning hands in a short period of time. Many players irrationally fear a player who's on a rush. If you've won a series of pots, especially if some of them have been showdown hands, you'll be seen to be on a rush. Consider loosening a bit, especially in unraised pots, if the players yet to act have significantly smaller stacks than yours. This is because players fearing your rush might pass some hands they would ordinarily play.

When facing a player who's on a rush, we recommend playing your normal strategy, or even loosening a little, because the player may be playing weaker-than-normal hands while "playing his rush." This could be a good opportunity to catch him with a weak hand and double through him.

DRY POTS

A dry pot is one with an all-in player. Therefore, the hand is guaranteed to go to a showdown. Unless you have a hand that is likely to beat the all-in player, it's a mistake to bet at a dry pot, unless there's a significant side pot. For example, a player with a short stack goes all-in for an amount equal to the blind. You have 7♣6♥ in the BB and get a free flop of A♣-5♦-4♥. If there are other players involved, there's no reason to semi-bluff at this pot, as it's highly unlikely you have a better hand than the all-in player at this point. If you make your straight, bet it and perhaps you'll get paid off.

Part Four

Advanced
Kill Phil Strategies

10

KILL PHIL EXPERT

If it wasn't for luck, I guess I'd win every tournament.
—Phil Hellmuth

After you've gained tournament experience and are familiar with the concepts discussed up to now in this book, you're ready to learn and implement more sophisticated moves. By combining these with what you've already learned, you'll be competitive in any tournament.

MAINTAINING STACK SIZE

Tournament experts constantly monitor their chip stack as it relates to the CPR. They want to avoid having their stack pared down to the point where it fails to significantly threaten other players. Though they'd prefer to play aggressively, and primarily with solid hands, during the middle stages of a tournament when the cards aren't coming, they look for opportunities to pick up chips based on the situation rather than their hand. Here are three common examples.

Moving in Against Multiple Limpers

In a pot with several limpers, an experienced player can move in with any two cards, banking on the probability that limpers won't call a big all-in raise, and he's usually right. Opponents are concerned that if they call, they'll be looking at a premium hand and could be a 3- or 4-1 underdog. Hence, they usually pass.

Should this attempted all-in coup get called, the pro is far from an automatic loser. Say he's moved in with a hand such as 8♦7♦ and is called by A♣K♠. He's slightly less than a 7-5 dog. This means he'll "get lucky" and double up 5 out of 12 hands. True, he'll be out of the tournament in similar situations 58% of the time, but the likelihood of picking up the bets from all those limpers, combined with his chance of doubling up if called, justifies this move.

The Power Re-Raise

Against a pre-flop raise from middle-to-late position followed by a call, an expert may make an all-in re-raise, knowing that the initial raiser has to not only worry about this fearsome raise he's facing, but also consider the player yet to act behind him. Top players know that if they can force the opening raiser out, the caller will almost always fold (unless he was slow-playing a big pair). The majority of the time, the first raiser will have a hand like AQ, AJ, a middle pair, or connectors, and will muck it in the face of such a powerful bet. The expert will pick his spots to make this type of play, selecting moments when it's most likely to succeed.

One player who loves to make this move is Barry Greenstein, a great poker pro known as the "Robin Hood of Poker," because he donates all his tournament winnings to charity. Late in a big tournament, there was a pre-flop raise and a call before the action got to Barry. He re-raised 400,000 and both players folded. Barry held 95 off-suit! He'd picked his spot well and added over 100,000 to his stack.

A move like this is very difficult to pick off. You'd feel pretty stupid risking all your money with a medium pair, or AQ, when there's an excellent chance you'll be looking at aces or kings. Even AK shrinks up in a spot like this. You're a 13-10 underdog against pocket 10s through queens, a 7-3 dog against pocket kings, and you need a doctor if he's holding pocket rockets. Do you really want to get involved? Although many Internet players call in this spot with AK (or even AQ or AJ), few seasoned tournament players would. They know that the only hand they'd like to see is an ace with a kicker weaker than a king; they also know it's unlikely that a player would make a huge re-raise with this type of hand. Unless they have a good read and are convinced that it's a bluff, it's tough to call with AK.

What makes this play so powerful is that players who make it will play their big pairs the same way. Top players have long memories and once they see someone move in with aces or kings in this scenario, they're unlikely to forget. In the past, few realized that players make moves like this, but extensive television coverage is now revealing some of the secrets of power no-limit poker.

Aggressive Stealing and Re-Stealing

A third way that experienced players attempt to maintain their chip position is by selectively increasing steal attempts, often with all-in bets. Against timid players, they might move in with any two suited cards. Against aggressive players who routinely raise in the steal positions, they might come over the top. In both cases, they hope to win the pot right there. But if they're called, they can still get lucky and double up. Situational play is a key ingredient in maintaining stack size throughout the tournament.

KILL PHIL IN THE LATE STAGES

One of the drawbacks of the Kill Phil strategy is that practitioners fortunate enough to garner a lot of chips late in a tournament frequently go into a shell, due to the lack of qualifying hands. This results in the blinds and antes eating away at our stacks until we've sacrificed our advantage.

This point is well-illustrated by Blair's recent experience when playing in a $100-buy-in NLH tournament on Ultimatebet.com. Late in the tournament, Blair, experimenting with KP Basic Plus, had a huge stack and was the chip leader with only 25 players left out of a starting field of 180. Following the huge-stack strategy, he went from first to eighth without playing a single hand. Analysis revealed that Blair had missed a number of opportunities to steal the blinds and antes, and when faced with a mini-raise, had folded some playable hands. Below are some strategy modifications that help rectify this situation.

Stealing

Consider becoming more aggressive with a huge stack. Once about half the players in the tournament have been eliminated, KP Basic Plus players with a huge stack should consider raising to five times the big blind from the cutoff, button, or small blind, with Group 1-9 hands. The size of this raise, combined with the threatening size of your stack, should convince foes to fold most hands. This play is most effective if the players yet to act after your raise have small-to-medium stacks. Remember, though, that players with very short stacks may call out of desperation. This is particularly true when the desperado is in the big blind. If he has only the amount of the blind left, or a little more, he'll be getting better than 3-1 odds on his remaining chips, and is correct to call with anything. In that case, limit your play to Groups 1-5 and 7.

When making this move, pay particular attention to the stack sizes of your opponents. If your bet of five times the big blind will force them to commit more than 1/3 of their chips, they'll probably be pot-committed. Should one of them decide to play, he's likely to either re-raise all-in pre-flop or move in on the flop. In situations such as this, it's better for you to make an initial raise sufficient to put your opponents all-in before the flop. By doing that, you take away any hope they may have had that you'll fold to a re-raise or post-flop bet, perhaps inducing them to fold a hand better than yours. It's often best to calculate an amount to raise that's greater than the largest chip stack of your opponents, rather than make an all-in bet.

Suppose you have 200,000 and your remaining opponents have 35,000, 30,000, and 25,000, respectively. With blinds of 2,000-4,000, it's passed around to you in the cut-off. You decide to try to pick up the blinds with 9♦7♦, a Group 9 hand. You correctly realize that the recommended raise of five times the big blind (20,000) will pot-commit any caller, so you decide to apply maximum pressure by forcing them to play for all their chips. If you raise 35,000-40,000, it's effectively the same as moving all-in.

Paradoxically, though, this bet is often perceived as stronger than an all-in move, which seems more like a steal. The other players will realize when they compare their stack size with your bet that it puts them all-in. Now it'll occur to them that you could have just moved in, but you didn't. Why not? It seems as though you're attempting to look less threatening, while still raising all their money. This can be really scary. It looks like you're inviting a call by not moving in. Most opponents will muck all but very strong hands and your steal will usually be successful.

Playing Against Another Large Stack to Your Left

Against a good aggressive player with a large (big or huge) stack on your left, you must alter your stealing strategy. Many players of this type will call your pre-flop raise, looking to trap or outplay you. This puts you in the unappealing predicament of playing small ball against an expert who has position. The safe route is to adhere to the basic strategy, but this may result in your anteing off until you reach medium-stack status, thus negating the advantage of having a lot of chips.

We suggest an alternative strategy in this case. Employ the medium-stack unraised-pot strategy. This means moving in instead of making smaller raises that leave you exposed to tough post-flop decisions. In raised pots, however, stick with the basic strategy. Don't employ this tactic all the time with the lower hand groups, just often enough to pick up sufficient blinds and antes to maintain your stack while waiting for a big hand. The big stack on your left needs a very strong hand to call. This gets back to the foundation of the KP strategy. You'll also be active enough that players will notice and may incorrectly call when you have a big hand. If the player to your left happens to pick up a big enough hand to call, you could get broke, but at least you went down fighting. If you happen to win, you've acquired a monster stack—and perhaps bagged a Phil in the process.

Defending Against Mini-Raises

One of the more effective plays used by experts when the blinds and antes are high is making a mini-raise of about twice the big blind. With blinds of 100-200, making it 400 to 500 to go is considered a mini-raise. These small unrevealing raises are often sufficient to pick up the blinds and antes, while not committing the raiser to playing the hand through. If re-raised, he can get away from his hand, unless he's loaded for bear, in which case he can either move in or trap the re-raiser post-flop for all his chips. Mini-raises are deceptive, concealing the strength (or weakness) of the raiser's hand, while also frequently winning the pot pre-flop.

Basic strategy doesn't distinguish between a standard raise and a mini-raise—a raise is a raise. However, once you've progressed to this point in your poker education, you may begin to pick up differences in the way certain players use mini-raises. As previously mentioned, if this type of raise is out of character for a particular player, warning lights should start flashing. Good players try to determine the minimum raise required to pick up the blinds and antes at their table. If only a mini-raise is necessary to accomplish this task, they'll become chronic mini-raisers. You can't allow a persistent mini-raiser on your right to force you into folding what would normally be playable hands. This is especially true when you have a huge/big stack and basic strategy calls for playing very few hands in raised pots. With a medium stack, the situation isn't nearly as limiting, since the universe of playable hands is increased. The short-stack strategy is fine as is.

Against a persistent mini-raiser, alter your strategy according to your stack size as follows.

Short Stack—No change.

Medium Stack—Increase the hands that you move in with by one Group in each position (i.e., if the strategy calls for moving in with Groups 1-3 versus an early-position raiser, revise this to Groups 1-4) when faced with a frequent mini-raiser.

Huge or Big Stack—Use the strategies that follow against a persistent mini-raiser, mixing up your play between the options given.

• Against an early-position raise, either smooth-call or move in with Group 1-2 hands. With Group 3 or 4 hands plus any pair, just call. Be prepared to pass on the flop if your opponent bets, unless you flop a set or have an over-pair to the flop, in which case vary your play between making a pot-sized bet or raise and moving in.

• Against a mid-position mini-raiser, vary your play between moving in and smooth-calling with Group 1-3 hands. Call with any pair or suited connector. Move in post-flop with top pair or better. If you flop a set, vary between moving in and slow-playing.

• Against a late-position mini-raiser, vary between moving in and calling with Group 1-4 hands. Call with small pairs and suited connectors. Use the advanced post-flop strategy.

To further vary your play and discourage a chronic

mini-raiser, consider occasional re-raises to six to seven times the big blind with Group 1-8 hands. If called and you're first to act, move in post-flop with top pair or better or any straight or flush draw. If last to act and your opponent checks, move in with any pair or better or with straight or flush draws. If your opponent bets, move in with top pair and top-kicker, or better; otherwise fold.

Limping

Earlier in the book we discussed limping with aces. We've also discussed all-in raises in certain situations against multiple limpers. Now that you're more experienced, it's time to consider limping, rather than folding, in late position—especially when you have a huge/big stack—with any pair or suited connectors when at least one limper has already entered the pot. You might also, on occasion, consider limping, rather than raising all-in when basic strategy calls for it, with Group 3 and 4 hands (88, 77, 66). In these instances, you're obviously hoping to hit a big flop and break someone without jeopardizing too many chips in the process. Plays like this make more sense when you have a huge/big stack than when you have a small-to-medium stack. The smaller your stack, the more inclined you should be to move in, which is what the strategy calls for. With a lot of chips, you're less inclined to put the entire stack at risk. You're more interested in seeing lots of relatively cheap flops in hopes of busting other players or flopping a big hand and winning a huge pot from another big stack.

Limping can be an effective strategy from late positions or the small blind early in a tournament in situations where the basic strategy calls for folding. As your poker skills increase, especially your feel for post-flop play, limping will become a potent weapon. Make adjustments to this strategy accordingly.

Post-Flop Trapping

We've already discussed post-flop trapping with big pairs. As a KP Expert player, you'll be involved in more pots post-flop with smaller pairs and connectors, thus you'll have more trapping opportunities.

As we've discussed previously, if you flop a set or top two-pair, the more unconnected the board, the safer it is to trap. That's because, in an unconnected flop, the turn card is much less likely to make your adversary's hand a winner. For example, if you have pocket 7s and the flop comes Q-7-2 rainbow, there's no turn card that will give your opponent a straight or a flush. It's unlikely he has more than two outs to make a better hand. This is an ideal trapping situation. By following our recommendations, you'll generally have last betting position post-flop, so you'll get to react to your opponents. If he checks, check back. If he bets, smooth-call and make your move on the turn.

Mixing Up Your Play

We've discussed a number of ways to mix up your play. We want your opponents to fear you. (The Phils use the intimidation factor to steal pots at will from awed opponents who are afraid to get involved with them.) Your early all-in moves are a great start toward fear creation. Unpredictability is another essential component. The more unpredictable you are, the more players will hesitate to get involved with you. Mixing up the way you play certain hands keeps your opponents off-balance. They won't be able to put you on a hand based on the size of your bets.

If you always move in with medium pairs, but always limp with aces, alert competitors will soon recognize that you have a very strong hand every time you limp. By varying your play—sometimes limping with small pairs and sometimes moving in with aces—your incongruous behavior is likely to create intellectual dissonance in your opponents, impairing their ability to analyze your play. Good! Keep them guessing.

In-the-Money Big-Stack Considerations

The important principle of avoiding other big stacks should remain a guiding force after you've made it to the money and are moving up the payoff ladder. As players get eliminated, your prize money grows. Patience is well-rewarded. Stay focused on attacking the short stacks, while avoiding the big ones. A loss of focus can be quite costly, as the following example illustrates.

In the 1993 WSOP Main Event, only three players remained. Jim Bechtel, with 1,150,000, had a slight lead over John Bonetti, who had 935,000. The third player, Glenn Cozen, had only enough chips left to survive a few rounds of blinds and antes. Cozen had been short-stacked the entire time at the final table, but had masterfully managed to maneuver around and stay alive. Then, this hand came up.

Bechtel, on the button, raised to 35,000. Bonetti called from the small blind. Cozen, with 55 in the big blind, had a decision to make. He could fold, move in and hope to win a race, or call and see the flop, which is what he chose to do. The flop was K♠-6♠-4♦. Bonetti and Cozen both checked. Bechtel bet 85,000. Bonetti raised to 180,000. Cozen, realizing that a fight was brewing, quickly folded and sat back, hoping to watch some fireworks. Bechtel, after considerable thought, just called. The turn brought the J♠. Bonetti quickly went all-in. Bechtel thought briefly about the possibility that Bonetti had made a flush, then moved his chips to the center. His call was made easier by the fact that, even had he lost, he would still have Cozen out-chipped almost 3-1. Bonetti showed A♦K♣, but Bechtel had a set with his pocket 6s and Bonetti was out. Just like that! The difference between second and third place was more than $200,000. Cozen still had a smile on his face when he was knocked out a couple of hands later.

In our view, the big stacks should have avoided this sort of confrontation until Cozen was eliminated—there was just too much money on the line to risk getting involved until that tiny stack was history. Had the two players with big stacks focused on eliminating the small stack before locking horns, they'd have both had far more equity. In this case, the reward for avoiding confrontation with each other outweighed the value of their starting hands. In our opinion, the mistake was Bonetti's check-raise on the flop. He turned a potentially small pot into a big confrontation. Had he chosen to play small ball, he very well might have lost only a small pot. The threat of a flush when the flush card hit on the turn would have forced Bechtel to exercise caution. Additionally, had Bonetti just called, Cozen might have put the rest of his chips in and been eliminated right there. By forcing a big pot, he jeopardized all his chips and it cost him more than $200,000 in prize money.

REVERSE TELLS

In KP Basic, we discussed tells and how you can regiment your behavior in order to reveal as little as possible to your astute foes. Let's take this a step further, considering subtle ways to send false signals that might convince your opponent that you're weak when you're actually strong, or vice versa.

Sophisticated players are constantly scanning their green-felt terrain looking for clues to support their decision-making processes. False clues may lead to an inaccurate perception. Anyone who's seen the movie *Rounders* is familiar with the classic hand between Erik Seidel and Johnny Chan at the 1988 WSOP main-event final table. In heads-up action, Chan flopped the nut straight and patiently and persuasively set a trap for Seidel, using a series of false tells to lure him in. Chan looked tentative, concerned, and indecisive. Convinced that Chan was weak, Seidel moved all his chips in with a single pair and, in the blink of an eye, Seidel was relegated to a second-place finish. Chan did a magnificent acting job and Seidel fell for it hook, line, and sinker. This scene has become the most viewed sequence in real-time poker, and it's the false tells that make it so memorable. (It's possible to get the wrong impression of Erik Seidel from watching this clip; he's one of the best and most respected no-limit hold 'em tournament players in the world.)

Because good players will probably pick up on the fact that you're inexperienced, reverse tells are likely to be effective. Good players pride themselves on their ability to read people. In fact, it's their main weapon against a player using the KP basic strategy. This is why we emphasize that KP Basic players focus on making their actions routine to neutralize this weapon. Taking this a step further, correct use of reverse tells can convert the expert's reliance on reading players into a liability.

Becoming proficient in this area is a vital part of an advanced player's arsenal and well worth the time spent to perfect it. Practice in front of a mirror. Many of the best players do. Luring an opponent into making a mistake in a key situation could be the difference between an early out and the big payday. Players on the fence about a key decision against an unknown and obviously inexperienced player will have almost no choice but to let perceived tells be a deciding factor. If a known player made the same move, they'd be viewed with far more suspicion.

FEIGNING WEAKNESS WHEN YOU'RE STRONG

Here are some simple ploys you can use when you have a strong hand, have made an all-in bet, and want your opponent to call.

Hold Your Breath

We previously advised you to make sure you keep breathing when you're being studied, because many players are too scared to move or breathe when they're bluffing. If you move in with a very strong hand, such as aces or kings before the flop, hold your breath for a count of 10-15 seconds, then breathe out as quietly and inconspicuously as possible. Don't sigh (see "Sighing" later in this section). Then hold your breath for another 10-15 seconds. Don't move a muscle. Try to emulate a startled deer caught in the high beam of a car's headlights—freeze. Don't fiddle with chips. Don't look around. If you feel a little starved for air due to the frequent lapses in breathing (a stare-down can last several minutes), don't worry about it. You may get a bit red-faced and look uncomfortable, but it's all part of the ruse. If you look like you're about to burst, your opponent probably won't be able to resist calling.

Cover Your Mouth with Your Hand

A liar has a tendency to cover his mouth with his hand. Try this when you have a powerful hand. It's one of the signs players look for when trying to pick off a bluff.

Re-Check Your Cards

If you're subjected to a long stare-down by a good player, you might re-check your cards, even though you know what they are. Say you have A♠K♠ and the flop is Q♠-J♠-2♠; your opponent bets and you move in. Now your foe stares you down. Re-checking your cards here might induce a call. Your opponent may incorrectly glean from this move that you're checking to see if you have a spade. If he has a hand, such as AQ or QJ, this move may separate him from his chips. It can also be used pre-flop with a big pair. The re-check may convince your opponent that you don't have a pair and are checking your suits. Players with big pairs rarely re-check their cards. A re-check is a sign of weakness. Whoops. Not!

Appear Indecisive

If an aggressive player has raised in front of you and you have a big hand, take your time and study awhile. Stare at your opponent, as if you're trying to pick up a tell. Start to call, then draw your chips back before you commit them, and stare some more. You may even throw in a small move that feigns throwing your cards in the muck. Don't overdo it. Just the slightest suggestion that you're about to fold is enough. Finally, reluctantly, call. Don't raise. You've now baited the trap. No matter what comes next, sensing your indecision, your aggressive opponent may try to blow you out of the water—much to his dismay.

About halfway through a no-limit hold 'em tournament, Lee encountered a situation that warranted deception. An aggressive player raised from the cutoff and Lee called on the button with K♣J♣. The flop was Q♣-T♣-9♣. Lee had flopped a straight flush! Knowing he had an unbeatable hand, he quickly determined that the best way to extract full value was with an Academy Award performance, and he feigned indecision. His opponent led at the pot and Lee immediately went into the tank. He intently stared at his opponent, nervously looking away when his stare was met. Then he counted out the chips required to call. Holding them in his hand, he moved as though he was calling, but at the last moment drew his hand back, staring at his opponent as if trying to get a reaction. Then with a subtle resigned look on his face, Lee picked up his cards a little and leaned a bit toward the muck, as you would if you were about to fold. After one final stare, he finally called. When the deuce of diamonds hit on the turn, his opponent, holding KQ, quickly moved all-in and was eliminated.

Lee noticed that a well-known player had taken all this in. Much later in the tournament, he used the same ploy against this observant player, but with a twist. After a preflop raise by the veteran, Lee went through an abbreviated version of the same routine. Then, with a what-the-hell attitude, moved all-in. The player quickly folded, undoubtedly believing that he was cleverly avoiding a trap like the one he'd seen set earlier, only this time Lee was on a total bluff with 83 off-suit! What had first been used to indicate weakness was now used to indicate strength—the old double reverse.

CONVEYING STRENGTH WHEN YOU'RE WEAK

Sighing

Inexperienced players with strong hands sometimes sigh in an attempt to look weaker than they are. This is a well-known tell, so sighing is usually interpreted as strength by well-schooled players. Sighing when you're weak can therefore be used as a reverse tell against good players.

Smiling

If you can teach yourself to smile genuinely when you're weak, it'll work to your advantage. A genuine smile or chuckle when you're faced with a stare-down will usually be interpreted as a sign that you're not bluffing. Bluffers are generally too scared to smile legitimately. If you know an amusing tidbit you can access in these situations that brings a smile to your lips, this may be helpful.

Reverse tells can be key assets in winning tournaments, but you must be sure not to overuse them. Good players have long memories. Once they've seen a kabuki-like performance, they won't forget. In such a case, you'll need to take the charade up a notch, as Lee did in the prior example. Mind games become an important part of top-level poker. But for now as an unknown player, the judicious use of simple reverse tells should prove profitable.

VERBAL PLOYS

Poker is meant to be fun. Part of the charm of playing is getting to meet, and enjoy the company of, new people. You encounter all types of personalities, from the outgoing and outrageous to the quiet and reserved.

There are many reasons to be affable and easygoing at the table. For one thing, many players are there primarily for enjoyment. They know they don't have a realistic chance of winning (unless, of course, they've read this book), but they're willing to write off the cost as entertainment value. At his first table in the Big One in 2004, Blair sat next to a player who'd never played a live tournament, or even any form of hold 'em, in his life. He'd seen tournaments on TV, could afford the entry, and simply wanted to experience the scene. Blair went out of his way to be friendly to the player, as well as the other, obviously inexperienced, players he encountered. Players like these are the lifeblood of the pro and any serious player who doesn't make their experience as enjoyable and pleasant as possible just doesn't get it.

Another reason to be friendly is that one of the weapons in a good player's arsenal is the verbal ploy. Again at the 2004 WSOP, Blair was into the third day of the final event. The only person he knew at the table was Alex Brenes, a very good player from Costa Rica, who was seated immediately to Blair's left. Blair was in the small blind with 5♥2♥. A young player with a big stack had limped in from the one-hole. It was passed around to Blair, who wanted to take a flop without being raised. He acted like he wanted to raise, then looked at the limper, saying "your limping scares me." He did this for two reasons. For one, he wanted to misdirect his opponents as to the strength of his hand. But more important, he wanted to remind Alex, who's not above raising as a steal in that situation, that the limper could have a big hand. Alex considered raising for a long time, but finally just checked. The flop came with three hearts. The limper made a big bet, and Blair raised and won a much needed pot. We'll never know if his ploy really discouraged Alex from raising. But little things like this can sometimes make a big difference.

Amarillo Slim tells a story about a publicized poker freeze-out challenge he played against a well-known woman. Before the match began, Slim opined, "She's got a better chance of stuffing a wildcat into a tobacco sack than beating me!" After winning the match, he kept up the dialogue, "I could see her left titty thumping every time she bluffed." He later admitted that at the pre-match reception, he'd asked her how she liked her cocktail and she squealed, "I like it!" At one point during the match, when he thought she might be bluffing, he asked her how she liked her hand and she said "I like it," but in a different tone of voice. This may be Slim's fiction. But in a rematch, the woman, having learned a lesson, stayed silent and came out victorious.

Slim is a master of verbal ploys. If you ever play with Slim, don't get roped into "jawing" with him.

Many of the new-school poker pros use conversation to gain information. Daniel Negreanu and Erick Lindgren, for example, regularly try to chat with opponents during a hand to aid their decision-making process. Some players think they can lead them astray by responding. Unless you think you can out-fight a tiger in a burlap sack, we suggest you remain silent and expressionless.

DEALS

Due to the fact that the blinds and antes are often quite high relative to the average chip stack when only a few players are left, deals are frequently made at the final table. Typically, deals are struck between the last two or three players, but sometimes five or more players may be involved. The prize money in some tournaments is particularly top-heavy; when the casino has guaranteed a first prize, second place and beyond may get squeezed down significantly. This renders deal-making an attractive option: Spreading the wealth leaves less to the whim of short-term fluctuation—i.e., luck. Lee actually made a deal involving the entire final table in a tournament that had an inordinately high first prize. Half the prize money was chopped up before a single final-table hand had been dealt. Later, we'll show you how he got the best of this unusual deal, but first some discussion of the basics.

Not all tournaments allow deals. Deals are prohibited in all WPT tournaments and in most other televised events, because the quality of poker generally deteriorates rapidly when the money's been divided up and participants are playing only for a trophy and bragging rights. Some corporate sponsors forbid their players from deal-making. They want the advertising benefit that comes with winning; they also want their share of the big money (since most get a percentage of the money their players win). Tournament results and wins are public information easily checked by sponsors. Deals are often less easy to verify, and most sponsors don't want the added aggravation that comes with constant verification. It's much less complicated to direct their charges with the simple edict: "No deals." The British five-man poker-pro consortium known as the

"Hendon Mob" makes no deals. There are also several individual players who refuse to make deals, either on principle (they don't approve of the concept), because they've got plenty of money and enjoy the challenge of playing it out, or because they think they have an edge by forcing their foes into an uncomfortable situation.

Factors that are usually considered in deal-making include chip count, experience, and position at the table relative to a large big blind. Players seem more amenable to deals when they know the blinds are about to bite into their stacks than they are when the blinds have just passed them, and with good reason. Having already paid for the next round is a significant advantage when the blinds and antes are high.

When the remaining players agree to consider a deal in live tournaments, they usually request a short break. Online, the final table is frequently monitored by a staff member of the site. If all players agree to discuss a deal, they all push the "sit-out" button on their screens or the site temporarily stops play while discussions are in progress. Whether in live or online tournaments, it's important to convey the exact deal that's been agreed upon to management, so it can be ratified by all parties. This helps prevent misunderstandings. Online staff representatives are careful to get the specific consent of each participant, after which they distribute funds accordingly.

The Standard Formula

There's a widely used standard formula for deals. Say three players remain; first prize is $50,000, second is $35,000, and third is $20,000. Let's suppose that the chip distribution among the players is 50%, 30%, and 20%. Since all players will automatically get at least $20,000 for third place, this becomes the base amount of the deal. Each player starts by pulling $20,000 from the prize pool. The standard deal formula calls for the remaining $45,000 ($105,000-$60,000) to be distributed on a pro-rata basis. The player with 20% of the chips gets an extra $9,000 (total of $29,000), the player with 30% gets an extra $13,500 ($33,500), and the player with 50% gets an extra $22,500 ($42,500). This formula is generally considered to be equitable, and is often used. For example, it's what the online site PokerStars uses when players ask what's a fair deal based on stack size.

But is this formula *truly* equitable? Let's look at a hypothetical case with three players remaining and prizes of $50, $30, and $20. There's a total of 100 chips in play and they're distributed 80-10-10. The standard formula would pay 52-24-24. But first place pays only 50. This is clearly too generous, because no one deserves more than first-place prize money. So the standard formula is a good deal for the leader and a bad deal for the small stacks.

Our advice? You should absolutely suggest a deal based on this formula, but if, and only if, you're the chip leader or close to it. In this case, you're clearly getting the best of it. But if you're behind, we don't recommend that you accept a deal based purely on percentages, unless the other players are willing to sweeten it a little in your direction. Note that this problem doesn't arise when only two players remain. With two players, your chance of winning is proportional to your stack size and the standard formula is equitable. In contrast, equitable 3-player settlements are non-linear (see Appendix X for a chart of equitable 3-player settlements).

> **Key Point**: If you're in the lead, push for a deal based on the percentage of outstanding chips. If you're one of the short stacks, demand more than the standard proportional distribution.

To review, the guiding principle in deal-making is to try to get a proportional split based on chip position if you're a leader, but to negotiate for more than a proportional split when you're behind. Of course, how good a player you are also influences deal-making. Inexperienced players are probably well-served by giving up a little, while experts may demand a bit more than a proportional share to settle. Deal negotiations often revolve around who wants the deal most—e.g., who needs the money, who's tired, etc.

At the beginning of this chapter, we mentioned a deal involving Lee that involved the entire final table and half the prize money. As you'll recall, first place in this tournament was disproportionately top-heavy. Lee was the chip leader going into the final table. Another player proposed a proportional split based on chip position for half the total prize money, with the other half to be played for. Naturally, based on the ideas that have just been discussed, Lee enthusiastically endorsed the deal, and, after a bit of persuasion, all players agreed. Lee finished fourth in the tournament, but because of this deal, received more than the second-place finisher. Nice!

11

KILL PHIL
IN PRACTICE

Poker is 100% skill and 50% luck.
—Phil Hellmuth

Throughout this book we've thrown a lot of concepts at you. The best way to put it together, and illustrate the complete Kill Phil strategy, is to put the ideas to use in an imaginary tournament, played from beginning to end. Please note that this sample tournament uses the full-on KP Expert strategy, employing many of the advanced concepts from Part Four.

We'll use a structure similar to the WSOP championship event, with 90-minute levels. At an average of 30 hands per hour, this means that a 10-handed table will see about 45 hands dealt per level. We'll condense it to a four-day tournament, starting with 300 players, using sample hands to illustrate key concepts (consult pg. 68 if you don't follow the calculation of CPR and CSI).

Level 1

Blinds:	25-50
Your stack:	10,000
CPR:	75
CSI:	Huge (10,000 > 2,250)

At the early levels, new-school players are actively trying to build pots and get hold of chips. Most other players are content to play very tight, hoping to trap someone who overplays a hand. Our recommendation with a CSI indicating a huge stack (chip total greater than 30X the CPR) is to play only AA and KK, raising enough to give trapping-minded opponents the wrong price to call with speculative hands, such as small pairs—in this case, it means raising to about 1,500. While this may seem like overkill, it should keep you out of trouble. The goal is to get to the higher limits with most of your bankroll intact.

At 30 hands per hour and blinds of 25-50, your cost for this level is a little over 300. In our sample tournament, you get aces once during the first level. A player with K♦Q♦ raises to 175; you re-raise to 1,750, and he folds.

Level 2

Blinds:	50-100
Your stack:	9,900
CPR:	150
CSI:	Huge (9,900 > 4,500)

You pick up kings later in the level, raise to 1,500, and pick up the blinds, plus 100 from one limper.

Level 3

Blinds:	100-200
Your stack:	9,475
CPR:	300
CSI:	Huge (but on the cusp, 9,475 > 9,000)

Your stack at this point is typical for a Kill Phil player. Unless you get aces or kings and get action, you'll generally blind off 5%-10% of your starting bankroll before the big-stack strategy kicks in. You get no playable hands for about an hour and your stack drops to the big-stack category. Then, a hand comes up in which you have 99 in the cutoff. Ordinarily, the basic strategy calls for moving in in this spot, but there are several limpers including one from early position (see "Limping with Aces," pg. 138). You just limp for 200. The flop comes 9♣-5♥-4♥ and the up-front limper bets 900 into the 1,000 pot. The other players fold. You move in. After some consideration, your opponent calls, showing that he did, indeed, have AA. One factor in his decision to call was that he figured a player with a set wouldn't move in, but would rather call or make a small raise in that situation. He figured you for a draw, an overpair such as JJ or TT, or an outright bluff. This demonstrates how the KP philosophy of moving in with all hands, including the strongest, instills confusion in opponents. Your hand holds up.

Level 4

Blinds:	100-200/25 ante
Your stack:	16,500
CPR:	550
CSI:	Big (30X the CPR equals your chip

count; this calculation doesn't have to be rigid; play as huge or big, possibly mediated by other factors)

You get moved to a new table. You notice that you have the biggest stack at the table. The players in the first three seats to your left all have less than 10,000, including the player immediately to your left, who has about 6,000.

You don't play a hand for about three rounds, leaving you with 14,700. You're in the big blind when the player on the button, with about 9,000, raises to 700. Each time it's been an unopened pot to him prior to this, he's raised your blind and you've folded (the player on the button is correct in raising your blind every time in this situation if you fold everything but big hands). The small blind folds. You have 7♣6♣ and move in! It's unlikely your opponent has a hand he can call with. He folds A8 off-suit and you pick up a decent pot, increasing your stack to 15,750. Additionally, your action will likely make him leery of making this play in the future (see "Is He a Bully?," pg. 108).

A little later, you raise to 1,400 on the button with 77 (see "Variations to Basic Strategy" #2, pg. 96), successfully picking up the pot.

Nothing eventful happens for the rest of that level.

Level 5

Blinds:	150-300/50 ante
Your stack:	15,000
CPR:	950
CSI:	Big (15,000 > 9,500)

Your table has been relatively calm. Four of the players are obviously nervous and inexperienced. They're playing passively and seeing their stacks dwindle, as the two aggressive players are small balling them successfully. The three other players seem competent and solid, but aren't doing anything remarkable. The aggressive players generally get out of their way when they enter a pot. These aggressive guys are seated two to your right with 9,500 in chips and four to your right with 13,500.

You're in the big blind with A♥Q♥. Everyone folds to the button. Your previous all-in re-raise has him a little gun-shy, but aggression is his style. He can't afford to let this one instance put him off his game plan. He takes another shot, raising with K♣7♣. You return fire, moving in again. He slowly folds, exhibiting some obvious frustration.

Next time around, you have 9♥8♥ in the small blind. Your nemesis, who now holds A♣9♣ in the cutoff, is down to around 7,500. Your re-raising strategy has him flummoxed, so he decides to try a different tack, just limping. You also limp (see "Limping," pg. 157). The button folds and the big blind checks. The flop comes 9♣-8♠-4♦. You decide to set a trap (see "Post-Flop Trapping," pg. 158). Based on your observations, you're pretty sure he'll bet in the cutoff if it's checked to him (see "Playing the Player," pg. 106). You and the big blind check. He bets 1,600 into a 1,400 pot. This bet indicates he has a made hand and wants to make it expensive for drawing hands. You move in. He calls and you bust him!

The frustrations of playing against a Kill Phil player caused a good aggressive player to make a fatal error. Had he made a normal raise instead of limping in the last hand, you'd have folded. Moving in would have been a mistake, because your image had changed, and it was too likely that he'd have put you on a steal and called with a better hand than yours. Your best play in this situation was to take a cheap flop with a speculative hand (see "Table Image and Changing Gears," pg. 114). As it turned out, that's what you did and you busted a tough opponent.

Level 6

Blinds:	200-400/50 ante
Your stack:	24,500
CPR:	1,100
CSI:	Big (24,500 > 11,000)

You're deep into the first day and still have a big stack. The overall situation continues to be fairly calm, as no one who might pose a big threat has been moved to your table. Until now. The short stack on your left finally goes broke and is replaced by a notorious Phil with a stack bigger than yours. This super-aggressive player sees your chips and begins to drool. The bully has entered the schoolyard and it's time to fight! Or is it? You look at the tournament clock and see that only 45 minutes are left until the end of the day's play. Seats will be re-drawn tomorrow. You decide to stick to the strict big-stack strategy for the rest of the session and hope to get a favorable table draw the next day.

You'll eventually run into a bully that you'll have to fight, but for now, you have a reprieve. Your careful observation of details has allowed you to avoid an unwanted confrontation. You end the day with 22,000, which is above average.

Level 7

Blinds:	250-500/50 ante
Your stack:	22,000
CPR:	1,250
CSI:	Big (22,000 > 12,500)

After the re-draw, your new table looks like this: In the two seats to your left are unknown players with stacks of around 10,000 each. The player three to your left has 36,000. The next two players have around 15,000, followed by two known Phils, one with 32,000 and the other with 33,000. The two players to your right are unknown and seem to be inexperienced from what you can gather watching their actions and talking with them (see "Playing the Player," pg. 106). They have 10,000 and 12,000, respectively.

You don't get much room to operate. The Phils are bullying the table and small-balling each other. You pick up QQ and move in over a middle-position raise by Phil #2, picking up the pot and adding needed chips to your stack, which is now around 23,000.

In the big blind, you pick up 6♥5♥. The pot is unopened to Phil #1, who raises to 1,900. Phil #2 calls in the cutoff. This is a situation you've been waiting for (see "Maintaining Stack Size," pg. 149). You figure that if you move in, it's highly unlikely that either Phil will call without aces or kings. Given the fact that you've played only one hand so far today and you're unknown to them, they must give you credit for a big hand. Even if one of them has aces or kings and calls, you'll still win almost 25% of the time (see "The Value of Suited Connectors," pg. 72). You make the move. Both Phils quickly fold and you add more than 5,000 to your stack.

Level 8

Blinds:	300-600/75 ante
Your stack:	27,000
CPR:	1,650
CSI:	Big (27,000 > 16,500)

You're deep into the tournament. Over half the players have been knocked out. You haven't had a pre-flop race yet and you still have a big stack. So far, so good. One of the small stacks on your right has been knocked out by Phil #1 and has been replaced by a cocky player with 62,000, the biggest stack at the table. The two Phils and the player with the big stack are putting pressure on almost every pot. You're getting run over, waiting for a big hand.

The decision you face at this point is common for all players who find themselves with a big stack in the mid-to-late stages of a tournament. Do you play it safe, try to work your way up the money ladder, and hope for enough big hands to take you all the way? Or do you take the bull by the horns and try to accumulate a mountain of chips through aggressive play with less than premium hands? Not content to sit on the sidelines, you decide that it's high noon and time to fight the bullies (see "Huge or Big Stack," pg. 117).

You're pretty sure neither of the Phils is willing to race for all his chips without a big hand, but the player to your right is unpredictable and seems willing to gamble. With these three players to your right, you're in a position to win a lot of chips with an aggressive strategy and a little luck. You're aware of the fact that a big confrontation with one of these bullies could also abruptly end the tournament for you, but you understand this risk and have conquered your fear. You're ready for the inevitable battle that's brewing.

The player to your right has raised from late position in every unopened pot. It's passed to him in the cutoff and, on cue, he raises to 2,600. You have TT and move in, as called for by the basic strategy. He quickly calls and shows A♥Q♥. You're a 6-5 favorite and win the race. You now have 55,000, the biggest stack at the table, and have wounded the dangerous player to your right. (Note: If one of the Phils had the AQ suited, he'd have probably passed when faced with your all-in re-raise. He'd have reasoned that you might have him dominated with AK, or have a high pair, which would make him either a slight underdog or a big one. These aren't the type of odds a Phil cottons to, especially when a major portion of his stack is at stake.)

Level 9

Blinds:	400-800/100 ante
Your stack:	55,000
CPR:	2,200
CSI:	Big (55,000 > 22,000)

The two players to your left are hanging on with less than 10,000. They're outclassed and unwilling to get aggressive without a big hand. That makes them too predictable. You pick up the blinds and antes twice from the button in unopened pots by raising an amount greater than either one of their stacks (see "Stealing," pg. 153), once with A♣T♥ and again with 55.

The player to your left is knocked out by the guy on his

left, who climbs back to 19,000. The empty seat is filled by a player with about 22,000.

You limp on the button with K♣J♣ in a pot with three other limpers, plus the blinds (see "Limping," pg. 157). The flop is T♣-9♣-4♠. The big blind bets 5,000 into an 8,000 pot. Everyone folds to you and you move in. The big blind thinks for a long time, then calls, showing A♥T♦. Even though he has the best hand now, you're about an 8-5 favorite to win (see "Post-Flop Match-Ups," Appendix VI). But you don't make your hand, and now have 34,000.

You move in a few times with hands that are called for by the basic strategy, winning uncontested.

Level 10

Blinds:	500-1,000/100 ante
Your stack:	37,000
CPR:	2,500
CSI:	Big (37,000 > 25,000)

There are 60 players left and the last 50 win prize money. Your stack is below the average of 50,000. Don't be concerned. While position relative to the average stack is important, it's not necessary that you consider it when playing Kill Phil. The important measure is the chip-status index, and you still have a big stack. You can afford to wait and play the strategy.

The player on your right has built his stack up to 50,000. He's constantly making mini-raises in late position in unopened pots, such as this one. This is preventing you from stealing the blinds. He raises to 2,000. You have AJ suited on the button. Even though basic strategy calls for folding, you must do something to discourage him from continuing to make this play (see "Defending Against

Mini-Raises," pg. 155). You move in. He folds A♣4♣ and you say, "Those little raises aren't gonna cut it anymore" (see "Verbal Ploys," pg. 166). You pick up 4,500 and fire a powerful warning shot.

The very next hand, you pick up KK in the cutoff. This time a Phil raises to 5,500, the player on your right calls, and you move in. The Phil folds, but the other player calls with 99 in a spot where he would likely have folded if you hadn't given him that verbal jab on the previous hand. These are the little things that can change the course of a tournament. Your kings stand up and you increase your stack to 88,000.

Level 11

Blinds:	600-1,200/200 ante
Your stack:	88,000
CPR:	3,800
CSI:	Big (88,000 > 38,000, but still below huge-stack level of 114,000)

There are 52 players left; you're only two away from the money. You have the biggest stack at your table. The small stacks are hanging on, hoping for a payday. Other players are wary of your tactics, so you're able to steal the blinds and antes twice, picking up 14,000 before the player in the 51st spot is knocked out (see "Close to the Money," pg. 142).

The small stacks get much more aggressive once they're in the money, so you stay out of their way, waiting to pick up a hand that can stand a race.

You raise to 7,000 with A♥J♣ on the button in an unopened pot; the big blind, with 8,000, goes all-in with 44. You obviously call the extra 1,000, but lose the race. Your aggressive play earlier, picking up the blinds and antes, allowed you to lose this one and still have about the same size stack you had before that series of hands. Had you won the race, you'd have really improved your position, but you still have 86,000.

Level 12

Blinds:	800-1,600/200 ante
Your stack:	83,000
CPR:	4,400
CSI:	Big (83,000 > 44,000)

There are now 40 players left. You pick up A♣4♣ in the cutoff. The big blind has 52,000. You raise to 7,500 (see "Maintaining Stack Size," pg. 149). Everyone folds and you pick up 4,400.

Next time around, you again make it 7,500 to go from the cutoff with Q♥J♥. This time the big blind, with 52,000, calls. The flop is 8♥-6♥-2♠. He checks and you move in. He folds K♣Q♣. With 30 players left, you have 96,000, still within big-stack parameters. Play ends for the day.

The new table assignments, which are posted that night, present a problem. The Phil you avoided tangling with yesterday is again seated to your left, with one player in between—and he has almost 200,000. You must make some changes to your game plan.

Level 13

Blinds:	1,000-2,000/300 ante
Your stack:	96,000
CPR:	6,000
CSI:	Big (96,000 > 60,000)

You sit through about a round and a half, getting no playable hands. Meanwhile, the Phil is terrorizing the table, limping, or making small raises in most unraised pots, and calling a lot of reasonable raises when he has position on the raiser. He's won a lot of pots, never showing down a hand. His stack has grown to 250,000.

Having a bully on your left is a problem. Your strategy of picking up pots with less than all-in raises is hindered by his willingness to call a raise and attempt to outplay you after the flop.

Poker at higher levels requires constant adjustments in accordance with changing conditions. At this point, you're familiar with all the KP concepts and have faith in your ability to think like a poker player. Since the Phil has the advantage of being to your left and he's very talented at the style of game he's playing, you determine that your best strategy is to revert to the all-in move and to loosen your hand requirements somewhat. This shifts the pressure back on him.

Your stack has shrunk to 84,000. You pick up 77 in middle position and move in, as called for by the medium- (not the big-) stack strategy (see "Playing Against Another Large Stack to Your Left," pg. 154). You get no callers. A few hands later you pick up A♥K♦ in the big blind and again move in, re-raising the Phil who'd made a mini-raise to 8,000 from first position with 77. You pick up 15,000, plus the 4,000 you'd posted in the big blind. You now have 104,000.

On the button, you pick up A♥J♥. It's passed to you. Many pots are being passed around because of the threat the Phil poses. Players who would ordinarily try to steal pots with medium-strength hands are staying out of his way. You move in again. The small blind, with a stack of around 50,000, reluctantly folds. The Phil, now in the big blind, shoots you a menacing look, stacks up his chips as if ready to call, then slowly folds. Is he trying to intimidate you in an attempt to keep you from moving in next time? You bet he is! Phils hate to be upstaged by impudent up-starts.

The next hand you pick up Q♥J♥. While the big-stack strategy doesn't call for a move-in, you feel you're on a roll and move in again when it's passed to you. This is a mistake for a couple of reasons. First, your table image has changed in the last few minutes as a result of your moving in three times (see "Table Image and Changing Gears," pg. 114). Players are now suspicious of your tactics and are more likely to call with hands they would have folded had your image been that of a tight player. Second, while QJ suited looks like a promising hand, the hands you'll get called with could easily dominate yours. The button calls with A♣Q♦. You lose 50,000, reducing your stack to 60,000. Ouch!

Level 14

Blinds:	1,200-2,400/400 ante
Your stack:	60,000
CPR:	7,600
CSI:	Medium (60,000 < 76,000, but > the small-stack cutoff of 30,400)

There are 21 players left. Losing the previous pot took

you out of big-stack status for the first time all day. You still have enough chips to put a player without a big hand to a tough call, but you can't afford to wait very long and still maintain that advantage.

You have 5♥5♦ in first position. While the strict medium-stack basic strategy calls for a fold, you'll have to take the blinds the next two hands, and they're about to go up. If you were content to just move up the money ladder, you'd fold here. But you're playing to win and decide to stay aggressive. In this hand, you'll be in bad shape only if someone has a bigger pair behind you and calls your all-in bet. The cumulative chance of any of the remaining players having a higher pair is 31% (see Appendix IX for cumulative chance of 55 or better with 9 players yet to act). Your stack size and your first-position raise may induce some players to fold hands such as 66 thru TT. You move in and get called by the button, who has A♣Q♣ and a bigger stack than yours. Although you'd rather he'd folded, it's OK. You're a favorite to double up and have a shot at the big money. Your 5s hold up and you have a big stack again.

With 20 players remaining, table assignments are redrawn. Your new table has a different Phil who's holding about 200,000, but this time he's two seats to your right. The players to your left have smaller stacks than yours.

Level 15

Blinds:	1,500-3,000/ante 500
Your stack:	125,000
CPR:	9,500
CSI:	Big (125,000 > 95,000)

You go card dead for a while, blinding off about 25,000. An aggressive player in middle position with about 50,000 makes a small raise to 7,000. You've noticed that he makes a lot of these small raises, but backs down to any show of strength. You have 66 on the button. The basic big-stack strategy calls for a fold in this spot. But you're on the border of being a medium stack (see "CSI Adjustments," pg. 104), which calls for a re-raise here, and your opponent is likely to have a hand that he won't call with. You move in, he folds AJ off-suit, and you add 16,500 to your stack. Once again, your astute observation of your opponents' tendencies has paid off (see "Playing the Player," pg. 106).

Level 16

Blinds:	2,000-4,000/ante 500
Your stack:	116,000
CPR:	10,000 (don't forget to account for the short-handed table in calculating the CPR)
CSI:	Big 116,000 > 100,000)

Only 15 players are left. The average stack is 200,000, so you're quite a ways below average, but still close to the break point between big- and medium-stack parameters. Your decisions on which way to lean depend on other factors, one of which is that you're now playing 8-handed, which means the blinds come around quicker. Notice that the CPR is now based on 8 players. However, the adjustments for the blinds coming around more quickly are contained in the strategy. At this point, only the first player to act, in position 8, is considered to be in early position. If you're in position 8, use the early-position strategy. Positions 7, 6, and 5 are middle positions (as before); use the middle-position strategy. This also applies to the re-raising strategy when it comes to determining the position of the raiser.

The Phil on your right is playing solid poker. His raises are treated with respect and you've yet to see a hand of his shown down. He raises to 12,000. You have KK on the button and move in for your remaining 104,000. The Phil goes into the tank, staring at you intently. You want him to call with a weaker hand, so you go into reverse-tell mode (see "Reverse Tells," pg. 160). You hold your breath for 15 seconds, not moving a muscle, then breathe out as quietly as possible. Then, seemingly subconsciously, you cover your mouth with your hand. The Phil, having noticed your re-raise earlier, considers your body language and, since you're unknown to him, calls with A♥K♦. Your heavily favored hand wins and you double up to 214,000, solidly in the big-stack category. The Phil quietly shakes his head; he'll have to give you more credit in the future.

The 12 players left are divided into two tables of six players each. You're playing short-handed and must keep up the aggression, because the blinds are coming around more quickly. You employ the final-table/short-handed strategy (see "Final Table," pg. 85).

You pick up Q♣T♣ on the button. However, there's been a first-position limper, so you fold. The small blind, with a short stack, moves in. The limper calls, shows KK, and wins the race against Q♥J♥. Nice fold! There are 11 left. Your table is now 5-handed.

A player in the one-hole moves in for only 26,000. You call from the cutoff with A♣J♦ (see "Calling Raises During the Move-In Stage," pg. 119). He shows J♣T♥. Your hand holds up and there's a break to re-draw for the final table. Unbelievable! You catch your breath, mop your brow, pinch yourself to be sure you're not dreaming, and promise yourself that you won't succumb to fear and choke now. You vow to stay aggressive.

Level 17

Blinds:	2,500-5,000/ante 500
Your stack:	250,000
CPR:	12,500
CSI:	Big (250,000 > 125)

The average stack is 300,000. You're below average, but back to 10-handed, and you've still got a big stack. There's plenty of time.

The table composition is as follows. There are two Phils—the super-aggressive one is three seats to your left with 395,000, the other is two to your right with 290,000. Three players are known tournament regulars and four others, including yourself, are unknowns. Three players have less than 100,000, while the two players on your left have about the same size stack as you.

You decide to tighten up to the strict big-stack strategy until some of the short stacks get eliminated, which happens quickly to two of them. You're down to eight and have moved up on the pay scale without having played a hand.

You pick up JJ on the button and move in. The player in the small blind calls with AK off-suit. He has 120,000. You're a 13-10 favorite, but an ace flops and you lose, leaving you with 110,000. Your CSI is on the verge of dropping from big-stack status. You need something good to happen.

The very next hand, in the cutoff, you pick up AA—the first time since the first level. Three players limp in front of you. Your obvious play is to raise, but from earlier observations you know that this is a situation that the Phil in the big blind loves to exploit, especially with a big stack, such as the one that he has. You decide to take a big gamble and just limp. Sure enough, the Phil raises to 40,000. All right!

The Phil on your right, who knows that his fellow Phil doesn't have to have a big hand to make such a raise, goes all-in for 200,000. Yeah, baby—come on in, the water's fine! As you move in also, the Phil in the big blind quickly mucks, laughing as he comments, "Ain't no fun when the rabbit's got the gun." The other Phil shows AK suited. He'd been trapping also, but it was he who got caught. You win a major pot and have over 250,000. You're feeling good about the way you're playing and your confidence is growing. This is fun!

Level 18

Blinds:	3,000-6,000/ante 1,000
Your stack:	245,000
CPR:	17,000
CSI:	Big (245,000 > 170,000)

The aggressive Phil goes on a tear, eliminating two players and wounding the other Phil. He's dominating the table, though you've been staying out of his way. The two players on your left when the table started are gone, so the streaking Phil is now directly to your left.

Level 19

Blinds:	4,000-8,000/ante 1,000
Your stack:	205,000
CPR:	18,000
CSI:	Big (205,000 > 180,000)

Six left. You now revert to the final-table strategy. You have A♣Q♣ in the small blind. The Phil to your right moves in for 68,000. You call and beat his 44. You've bagged your first Phil, but there's another one hungrily lurking on your left. Better stay focused and alert.

With five players left, you have 268,000. The average stack is 600,000, but the stacks aren't equal. Starting with the player to your right, the chip counts are 325,000, 145,000, and 475,000, and the Phil has the remainder: 1,787,000.

Level 20

Blinds:	5,000-10,000/ante 1,000
Your stack:	255,000
CPR:	20,000
CSI:	Big (255,000 > 200,000)

With the Phil in such a dominating chip position, many players would basically concede first place to him and focus on moving up the money ladder. While this isn't an unreasonable course of action, that type of thinking often translates into tightening too much, which means you can take advantage by staying aggressive.

The Phil's in small-ball mode. He's making small bets and raises, which are highly intimidating to those struggling to hang on. However, he doesn't want to double anyone up by over-committing with a weak hand.

The only time you get to act after the Phil pre-flop is when you're in the big blind. You pick up 22. The Phil, under the gun with Q♥9♣, raises to 22,000. You move in after it's passed around and he folds. Your play is unlikely to cause him to change his game plan, but you pick up 32,000 and save your 10,000 big blind, as well.

The next hand you're in the small blind. It's passed to you. You know that if you call, he'll raise, as he's done every time he's had that opportunity. You have A♣Q♣.

Moving in here will probably win the pot, but you want more. You call. On cue, he raises 28,000 more and now you move in. He sighs, obviously perturbed that you aren't following his script, but loathe to back down repeatedly to an insignificant unknown player like you. The Phil calls with A♠J♦. You win and suddenly have almost 600,000!

The short stack is busted after putting in his last 90,000 with A♣3♥ from the one-hole and running up against the Phil's A8 (see "Rounding Up the Desperado," pg. 120).

You're following the final-table strategy, moving in often. The Phil and the other players have stayed out of your way and your stack has climbed to 680,000. The Phil is dominating the pots you don't play and the other stacks are shrinking. The players to your right have 265,000 and 340,000, respectively. The Phil has 1,715,000. You'd like for one, or both, of the smaller stacks to get knocked out, but you've decided not to tighten while you wait for that to happen. You keep playing your game.

You pick up J♥T♥ on the button. The strategy calls for moving in, but you pause. From ongoing careful observation, you're aware that the player in the big blind looks at his cards as soon as he gets them. You notice that he has shifted noticeably in his seat, sitting up straighter. He's visibly nervous. You decide he has a real hand and wisely fold. The Phil calls in a spot where he would usually raise. Something's amiss. The big blind moves in and the Phil calls quickly with QQ. The big blind shows TT. And now there are three!

The chips counts: You 710,000. The Phil 2,050,000. The other 240,000.

You suggest a deal. You might not get the best of it here, but as a less experienced player, you should be willing to settle for any deal that's close to fair. The Phil declines.

Level 21

Blinds:	6,000-12,000/ante 2,000
Your stack:	710,000
CPR:	24,000
CSI:	Big (710,000 is just below the huge-stack cutoff of 720,000)

Again, your choice is to stay aggressive to maintain your best chance of winning or to tighten up until the other player is eliminated. Luckily, your dilemma is short-lived. The short stack goes all-in from the button. You call with A♥K♥, which dominates, and beats, his AJ off-suit.

The Phil has you out-chipped 2-1. You again offer a deal. Again he refuses. "OK, don't say I didn't offer," you reply with more bravado than you really feel. Once again, you remind yourself to stay aggressive.

The first hand, he has the small blind on the button. He raises to 30,000. You ponder awhile, then move in. He folds. You continue to move in every hand, regardless of what he does, for the next nine hands. You've picked up around 200,000. Next time he's on the button, he just limps. You find this suspicious, since you know he knows you're going to move in. So you check with 9♣6♦. The flop comes 6♥-4♣-2♠. You check, he bets 20,000, and now you move in. He folds A♣K♦. (Note that this type of play wasn't discussed in the text. However, our goal is for readers to become thinking skilled poker players. If you've assimilated all the concepts we've covered, you should be capable of formulating plays like this.)

"What's that you were saying about a deal?" the Phil says quietly (see "Deals," pg. 168).

Tournament Summary

While the outcome of the sample tournament is certainly contrived, the possibility of such a result is real. For any player, regardless of skill level, to win a major tournament, he must survive several races. The more races you can avoid, the more the luck factor is reduced. The more proficient you become at applying the Kill Phil strategies, the more pots you'll win uncontested.

Mastery of all the Kill Phil concepts should enable you to play at the level portrayed here. Once you've reached this point, you'll have a solid platform on which to incorporate a solid small-ball game. The more proficient you become at small ball, the more powerful your overall game becomes. Just remember, Kill Phil is your foundation. Don't abandon what you've learned here.

12

ATTITUDES AND LATITUDES

Chance favors only the prepared mind.
—Louis Pasteur

INSIGHTS AND OBSERVATIONS

To develop the Kill Phil strategy, we matched up hands against various plausible calling strategies to compute expected values.

> **KEY POINT**: The optimal all-in raising strategy is dependent upon which hands an opponent is likely to call with; similarly, the optimal calling strategy is dependent upon which hands a competitor is likely to raise with.

If your opponents change their calling strategies, you should change your raising strategies. It's something like a teeter-totter—both sides go up and down until an equilibrium point is reached. Based on our tournament experience, we made assumptions as to what hands a typical player would likely need to call an all-in wager. We then adjusted the figures a bit to account for probable adjustments experienced players might make in their calling strategies, and for purposes of simplicity. The basic strategy isn't perfect, but it's a reasonable approximation based on tournament conditions KP players are likely to encounter.

If a given player's raising or calling requirements differ significantly from the norm, the optimal corresponding calling or raising strategy also changes. An amusing anecdote illustrates this concept in practical terms.

In a super-satellite for a $10,000 seat in the 2003 Aussie Millions main event, Lee had a medium stack and was in the big blind. An aggressive British player on the button, who had Lee well-covered in chips, raised an amount equal to half of Lee's stack. The small blind passed. Lee's hand was Q♣9♣. He pondered awhile, sensed that the raiser was weak (he observed, and correctly interpreted, a tell), and moved in. The raiser, getting more than 3-1 pot odds, appropriately called and showed 63 off-suit. When Lee turned over his Q9 suited, the raiser was incredulous and asked, "How can you call with Q9?" Lee replied, "Because I knew you could raise with 63!" (As another player pointed out, Lee actually didn't call he raised. Lee realized he would be pot-committed if he called and, being out of position, decided to move in pre-flop.)

While working on the strategy, we were able to form some interesting general observations about the KP system.

1. It's usually correct to loosen your raising strategy when your opponents play tight and to tighten your rais-

ing requirements as your opponents loosen. The optimal strategy shows great sensitivity to such changes.

2. The correct raising strategy is not significantly different when there are many players left to act. There's little difference between nine players acting after your raise, as opposed to seven players. But when three or fewer players are left to act, the raising strategy changes dramatically (assuming that all remaining players have the same calling strategy). The fewer the remaining players, the more hands you should raise with. This effect is especially pronounced when on the button and in the blinds. Here, for example, if your opponents are tight and call only with the top 20% of hands, with a medium-to-small stack you should seriously consider raising all-in with any two cards! In this situation, most of the money you make comes from stealing the blinds and you're a favorite to do so. If you're not called, it doesn't matter what two cards you have. With a small-to-medium stack, moving in from the button or the blinds with any two cards against tight players is the correct play. We don't recommend this play for beginners who may have difficulty distinguishing between tight and loose competition, but it's an important adjustment to the basic strategy for advanced players to make.

3. The all-in or fold recommendations for after another player has raised are based on assumptions we made regarding which hands a typical player would raise with, depending on position. Stack size of the raiser is also taken into consideration in KP Basic Plus. Please note that these aren't the correct calling strategies against a Kill Phil player. We don't discuss these for obvious reasons.

How does our strategy stack up against other strategies

designed for relatively inexperienced players? Howard Lederer presents a strategy for beginners in his DVD, *Secrets of No-Limit Hold 'Em*. His strategy is designed to be tight to keep beginners out of trouble on the flop. He recommends playing up to the top 12.5% of hands, depending on position.

The KP basic strategy has you playing up to 36% of the hands, depending on position and stack size. Similar to Lederer's system, it also keeps players out of trouble on the flop by eliminating the need for post-flop decisions in most cases. Lederer's recommended strategy seems appropriate as a flop-oriented beginner's strategy early in a tournament, but it seems to us that it's too tight later on, when the blinds and antes are high. Our concern is that players using this system won't find a sufficient number of hands to play and the blinds and antes will gobble up their stacks (unless they're fortunate enough to pick up a lot of big hands).

David Sklansky presents an all-in-or-fold strategy in his improved version of the *System*. It contains some excellent features and has both advantages and disadvantages relative to Kill Phil. It relies on dividing your stack size by the blinds (and antes, we assume), then multiplying this figure by the number of players yet to act, to arrive at what he calls a "key number." This number requires a further adjustment to account for limpers. This heuristic is particularly effective when the number of potential callers is small or when the stack size is huge; his *System* accurately reflects the effect of fewer callers on hand selection. We've accounted for this effect by making the cutoff, button, and blinds separate categories. Sklansky's *System* is superior to ours in evaluating the effect of huge stacks. We don't distinguish between a stack size of 33X the big blind (CPR of 3%) and stack sizes of, say, 50X the big blind or more.

We've compensated for this by recommending extremely tight play with big stacks.

Sklansky's *System* advocates playing up to about 50% of the hands, depending on position and stack size. We don't know what assumptions David used for calling strategies, which, as you now know, make a significant difference in determining the appropriate raising strategies. For example, with a stack size of 30X the blinds, raising from the cutoff with weak aces and kings is a losing proposition if the potential callers will call only with medium pairs, a big ace, or better (66 through AA and AT through AK). In such cases, Sklansky's *System* appears to be a bit loose.

One dramatic difference is in how we rate KQ. Sklansky ranks it in his top 6% of hands; we rank it in the top 12.5%. We don't rank it higher due to the risk, when called, of being dominated. Sklansky also doesn't distinguish between pairs 22 through 99. We rank medium pairs significantly higher (top 6%) than small pairs (top 12%). Medium pairs, such as 88, do much better than small pairs, such as 33, if opponents are likely to call with hands like 77 or A7 suited, as they often will against a late-position raiser.

Our systems also handle limpers differently. Sklansky tightens significantly when limpers are in the pot; we don't, except that we advise exercising caution when early-position limpers are involved. A couple of late-position limpers doubles the number of potential opponents, but also doubles the size of the pot. This makes stealing more lucrative. The effects are roughly offsetting. Also, since few players in middle-to-late position limp with high-medium to big pairs (99 through AA), AK, or AQ, few limpers are prepared to call an all-in raise.

Sklansky's improved *System* requires first dividing the sum of the blinds and antes into your stack size, then multiplying this number by the number of players yet to act, then again multiplying the product by the number of limpers plus one. In the heat of battle, these computations are near impossible to perform, especially for new players.

Naturally, you should use which ever system works for you and provides the best results. We think you'll find Kill Phil both powerful and manageable.

LUCK

How big a factor does Lady Luck play in no-limit hold 'em tournaments? To win tournaments, you've got to play well and you've got to get lucky in some key spots. Scotty Nguyen got lucky with AQ against the late Jack Keller's QQ on his way to winning the Big One in 1998. Chris Ferguson was all-in and covered, as a 4.25-1 dog, with pocket 6s against Jeff Shulman's pocket 7s, but caught a 6 on his way to winning the $1.5 million first prize in the 2000 WSOP main event. Everyone who's seen the ESPN tapes knows how lucky both Chris Moneymaker and Greg Raymer got in respectively winning the Big One the past two years.

Then there was this hand.

In the $25,000-buy-in WPT Championship event, Alan Goehring and Kirill Gerasimov were battling heads-up for the $1.5 million first prize. As the TV cameras revealed, Kirill had gotten away with some spectacular bluffs to chisel away at Goehring's huge chip stack and pull up to almost even in chips. On the key hand, both players saw the flop cheaply—Kirill with 86 and Alan with 85. The flop was 4-5-8, giving Alan top two pair and Kirill top pair and a gut-shot straight draw. Alan bet, Kirill moved in, and Alan quickly called. The winner of this hand would surely be the WPT champion and take away the lion's share of the dough. When the cards were exposed, Kirill looked sick, but despair turned to elation when the turn card brought a miracle 7, filling his inside straight! A stunned and dejected Goehring, who had never won a tournament, had one foot out the door when the river card was dealt. Unbelievably, it was the case 8, giving Alan a miracle re-draw and a full house! It was all over. Alan had won. You'll probably never see a more dramatic hand in such an important tournament, and luck certainly played a key part in the outcome.

Aggressive players who get lucky win tournaments. That's a fact. Their aggressive play often allows them to accumulate a big stack of chips, which permits them to withstand some losing confrontations and still have enough chips left to remain competitive. Then, relentless attacking tactics facilitate re-building their stacks. When they get lucky, often having the worst hand when they're finally called down, they're then positioned to make the final table, where continued aggression gives them a real shot to win. Luck plus aggression is a tournament-winning combination.

The goal of the KP strategy is to help a beginner win a tournament with the least amount of luck possible, even though he doesn't possess the skills required to fight tournament experts on their terms. You'll ultimately need to go all-in many times to win and you'll need to win a number of key races and showdowns. The KP strategy strives to minimize the cumulative risk in achieving your goals.

TOURNAMENT PREPARATION

We prepare for tournament play both mentally and physically. Lee, an M.D. (no longer practicing) with a special interest in human nutrition, exercise, and techniques for developing mental clarity and focus, approaches it with a focus and intensity that includes diet, supplements, exercise, and stress-reduction techniques.

Tournaments are a Series of Grueling Events

The WSOP, as well as most other major poker tournaments these days, are far more than a single event. There is no qualification process to get into the WSOP main event. You simply put up the money and take your seat. However, many don't realize that the complete World Series of Poker is a long series of separate events.

To prepare for an individual event is one thing; to be in shape to play well through an entire tournament is another. It's the difference between running a mile and a marathon. In the old days, tournaments were spread throughout the year, with ample time in between to rest and recover. No longer; the 2005 World Series of Poker kicked off in early June, and didn't finish until mid-July. That's a long time to play intense focused poker.

Blair, who had just turned 50, had good success at the 2004 WSOP, with three final tables and six cashes, including 54th in the Big One. Getting that deep into modern-day WSOP events, with their huge fields, requires putting in long hard days. For example, the $1,500-no-limit event started at noon on April 30th. Most events at major tournaments are now two-day affairs. The first day's play ended around 4 a.m. on May 1st, with 18 players remaining.

Play resumed that afternoon at 2 p.m. It took until nearly 9 p.m. to get down to the final table. Then, since it was an ESPN televised event, there was a break for interviews, as well as a quick bite to eat. After all that, it was time to play for the real money!

In the 2005 WSOP, with record-breaking fields in virtually all of the events, many of them took three full days to complete. And the WSOP is only one of a year-round schedule of major tournaments taking place throughout the world. Today's tournament professional must be truly well-conditioned if he hopes to compete on the tournament trail.

Focus

Focus is one of the keys to tournament success. Mistakes, or oversights, can be costly, if not fatal. Picking up tells and tendencies in your opponents can be lucrative. To optimize your chance of winning, you must have a clear mind and be attentive at all times. For this reason, we clear the decks prior to a tournament. This means other business, sports betting, and ongoing personal situations are set aside. We become mono-dimensional, clearing our minds of any and all distracting thoughts. To win a tournament, we know we must endure a 12-hour daily vigil that demands complete concentration. When others at the final table look tired and worn, we want to still be fresh, focused, and engaged.

No Cash Games

While we both regularly play cash games, both live and online, we never do so while competing in a long tournament. That's right, no live action for us during a tournament, and we advise you to similarly refrain. We don't think it's possible to be at our best in tournament play when we've spent time in cash games. First, the tactics required are very different and it's not easy to quickly switch back and forth. But more important, if tournament play is to be given the focus, attention, and effort it deserves, cash play is just too draining. We know players that go to tournaments and play only cash games. This, too, is a viable strategy. Cash games tend to be juicy at big tournaments. This is probably due to a combination of factors.

• The tendency of big tournaments to attract large numbers of players, many of whom are less than expert.

• Tournament players, whose skills don't translate well into cash games, often sit in if they're eliminated early from that day's event.

• Players skilled at both disciplines who attempt to play both are most likely playing each at less than maximum efficiency, due to stamina considerations.

When Blair began playing big tournaments, he couldn't make up his mind where to focus his efforts. As soon as he'd sit down in a tournament event, he'd canvass the lucrative side games, often wishing he hadn't entered that day. Then, if he skipped a tournament, he'd see the result sheets the next day and wish he'd played. There's so much action at major tournaments—the events themselves, side games, and satellites, not to mention the juicy golf action that accompanies many tournaments—that it's hard to commit to a specific area. Blair has learned over the years that it's necessary to commit. With the spotlight on tournament play these days, he's decided to concentrate on this area, and his results have mirrored his commitment.

Homework

If we know that certain players will be at a big tournament, we'll brush up on their tendencies by reviewing our notes and watching World Poker Tour or World Series of Poker DVDs. Beginners would be well-advised to carefully review "Kill Phil Basic," Chapter 7, before playing, and more advanced players should review "Kill Phil Basic Plus" and "Kill Phil Expert," Chapters 8-10. Additional reading may also be helpful in advancing your knowledge after you've mastered the strategies here (see "Recommended Reading and Web Sites," Appendix XI).

> **KEY POINT**: Mental and physical preparation improves tournament performance. The better prepared you are for peak performance, the better you're likely to do.

TOURNAMENT BURNOUT

The late stages of the first day of an event are very intense, with lots of adrenaline pumping. If you make it through, it may be very hard to wind down and get to sleep. Then you have to come back and play the final. Going through this scenario five or six times in the space of a month, as well as playing in other tournaments in which you don't get as far, can really tear you down if you're not in top shape. (And the WSOP main event is now nine days in itself!)

Blair has been around the poker scene for about 25 years. Yet, on the fifth day of the 2004 WSOP final, he arrived at his table to find no one he had ever played with (or had even seen) before. Moreover, he was the only one not in his 20s. Modern poker tournaments have become a young man's game—one for those who prepare properly.

TRAVELING

In poker, there's much to be said for home-court advantage. This is particularly true when contestants travel internationally to venues with significant time adjustments that can wreak havoc with their natural circadian rhythms. Due to tight scheduling between big tournaments, players frequently arrive in the middle of a series, in time to play only the last scheduled events, which have the biggest prize pools, the most prestige, and television coverage. Corporate sponsors, which a number of pros now have, strongly encourage their players to participate in televised events. This necessitates lots of travel.

Historically, players traveling long distances and entering the fray shortly after arrival have had sub-par results. American players journeying across the Atlantic to the WPT event in Paris have done poorly. At a televised event attended by many of the top American pros in Dublin, not a single one of them made the final table of the main event.

There are some steps you can take to combat jet lag and travel fatigue. First, if at all possible, it's good to give yourself a few days to adjust to the time change. Walking, swimming, or working out upon arrival is also helpful. Try to stay awake until around 9 p.m. in the locale you're in. Taking a long nap upon arrival is often counter-productive—you'll probably be up most of the night.

For the first few days, taking 1 mg of melatonin at bedtime helps re-set your body clock. Melatonin is the same substance produced by your pineal gland, responsible for regulating circadian rhythm. If you take it at bedtime, not only will you sleep better, but you'll shift your body's natural rhythm to put it more in concert with the new time zone. This is a trick used by many pilots and flight attendants.

If available in your area, we also recommend the homeopathic over-the-counter product "NO JET LAG." Taken as directed, this harmless product consistently reduces jet lag. Combined with melatonin at bedtime, it'll go a long way toward making you mentally able to play at your best wherever you choose to travel. Lee attributes this combination to the success he's had in international tournaments, making far more than his fair share of final tables.

ATTITUDE

Players with a positive attitude seem to consistently do better in poker, blackjack, and other forms of advantage play than players who think negatively. Most poker players can recall times when they've been "in the zone." During these periods, it seems that whatever they do comes out right. They consistently make the right play at the right time; their reads of opponents are uncannily accurate. Even when they're behind in a race, they're confident that they'll come out with the best hand.

We don't believe in ESP or the power of psychokinesis, but we firmly believe that it's beneficial to have a positive attitude. No-limit hold 'em is a game where power and perception make a difference. Players who exude confidence and go on a rush are generally feared by other players. Fear provides a fertile breeding ground for mistakes, and mistakes lead to missed opportunities and lost pots. Though a player's attitude may not be capable of manipulating the cards, it can certainly have an unnerving effect on the other players.

Confidence, success, and optimism can also lead to more focus. The more focused a player, the more likely he is to observe subtle nuances in the demeanor of opponents that can be exploited. Players who think negatively miss things. They're thinking about a bad beat or a bad run of cards and may overlook an important clue.

Optimistic players, on the other hand, generally have clear minds and sharp perceptions. They don't miss anything. Free from distracting thoughts, they're able to read micro-expressions in their opponents, gleaning information that can make a significant difference in their decisions. A micro-expression is a fleeting uncontrollable facial expression or alteration in body language subsequent to a stimulus, such as looking at a hand or a flop.

Sometimes players talk about having "intuition," which helps them determine if another player is weak or strong. You might hear someone say, "I knew he was bluffing. I could just feel it." Phil Hellmuth has said that he can look at an opponent and "see into his soul." Most probably, this "intuition" revolves around picking up a subtle change in their opponent's demeanor that they've observed, but are unable to verbalize. Positive thinking frees the mind and forms a basis for the mental clarity and focus required to grasp these subtle nuances and act on them accordingly. When they're right, as players in the zone usually are, their opponents become even more intimidated. Soon the focused player is running over the table, dominating play, and accumulating a massive stack of chips.

Does positive attitude make a difference? You can bet

on it! It may not turn you into a Kreskin, but it can be an integral part of the program that makes you a consistent winner.

RULES

At the advent of poker tournaments, written rules were minimal, if not non-existent. As tournaments became more popular and widespread, it became necessary to develop standard rules to cover situations unique to tournaments. Unfortunately, while most applications of rules are widely accepted, there are still no standardized rules in place at all poker tournaments. This is currently being worked on and, hopefully, a standardized set of internationally accepted rules will be established soon.

Players new to bricks-and-mortar tournaments, most of whom had previously played only online, often aren't aware of the rules and protocol of live-tournament play. As a result, they often make costly (or embarrassing) mistakes. Let's look at some of the common errors.

The String-Raise

The most common error is the "string-raise" (also referred to as a "string-bet"). The spirit of the rule is that a player wanting to raise must make his intention crystal clear. Before the flop, if a player puts an oversized chip in the pot, it's a call unless he says "raise" before the chip is put in the pot. For instance, the blinds are 50-100 and before the flop a player throws a 500 chip in the pot without saying anything. This can only be a call, regardless of that player's intention. Furthermore, let's say the player intends to raise, but states "raise" a second after the chip is tossed into the pot. This is also only a call. The intention must be stated *before* the chip hits the pot. To avoid disputes, these rules are necessary. They are, however, subject to potential abuse (see "Ploys of Questionable Ethics," pg. 222).

Another example is when a player wanting to raise puts the amount of the original bet in the pot, then reaches back to his stack for more chips without having stated his intention to raise. This will be ruled as just a call. In this case, if the player had declared his intention to raise before he put any chips in the pot, he would be allowed to put in a raise subsequent to pushing in the original chips. To take this a step further, let's say the player wanted to call a bet of 100 and raise 600. If he says raise without stating the amount of his raise, puts in the original bet of 100, then puts in 300, then goes back to his stack for 300 more, by rule he is allowed only a 300 raise.

To be safe, a player should put the entire amount of the call and raise into the pot in one motion. Or, to avoid any mistakes, clearly state the amount of the raise before putting any chips in the pot. The reason for this rule is to prevent a player from trying to gain an unfair advantage, known as "taking a shot," by gauging the reaction of players behind him before completing his action.

After the flop, if no one has bet in front of you and you throw in an oversized chip, unless you state otherwise, the bet is the amount of the chip. If you throw in a 1,000 chip and don't say anything, you've bet 1,000, regardless of your intention. However, if a player has bet in front of you, the rules are the same as before the flop—throwing in an oversized chip is considered a call. You must make your intention to raise, and how much, clear at all times.

Occasionally, a player makes a mistake in betting shortly after an increase in the blinds, failing to realize that there's been an increase. The general rule is that if 50% of the amount necessary to raise is put in the pot without the actual intention being made clear, that player must put in an amount equal to the minimum raise. For instance, if the blinds increase from 100-200 to 200-400 and a player puts in 600 (the amount of a common raise at the 100-200 limit), his only option is to put in another 200, constituting a minimum raise. If, however, he had put in 500, his raise would be disallowed and he would be allowed only to call the 400 blind.

Once you've announced your intention, you're required to follow through with it. If you state "raise," you can't change your mind; you must make at least the minimum raise. This rule can come into play in a few different ways. One of our pet peeves in tournaments is when dealers don't do their best to make the action clear to all players. Let's say a player on one end of the table throws in an oversized chip and quietly says, "Raise." The dealer says nothing and a player on the other end of the table who hasn't heard the player's declaration assumes that it's just a call. He declares, "Raise." Even though he might not have re-raised in this spot, he's now required to do so. He must put in at least a minimum raise. The proper way to handle this is for the dealer to state what he believes the action to be, loudly enough for the whole table to hear, as soon as the chips hit the pot. If the dealer is wrong in his assumption, the player has the obligation to correct him before there's further action, or the dealer's declaration stands. When an oversized chip hits the pot, there's often confusion. A lot of this can be eliminated if dealers are more committed to making the action perfectly clear.

Another example is when a player is raising as a bluff. He says, "Raise," but before he declares an amount or puts any money in the pot, an over-eager player behind him

says, "All-in." The first player will probably want to re-
tract his raise, but he will be required to put in at least the
amount of a minimum raise. (The minimum raise is one
equal to the amount of the previous bet. If a player bets
100, the minimum raise is 100, or a total bet of 200.)

Here's a situation that can be much more devastat-
ing to a player. A prime example comes from the 2004
WSOP. The blinds were 6,000-12,000. Doyle Brunson,
having around 100,000, announced, "All-in." Doyle was
committed to this raise, even though he hadn't actually put
the chips in the pot yet. Bradley Berman, because of some
commotion in the background, didn't hear Doyle's declaration and, not seeing any chips going into the pot, announced, "Raise." By rule, Bradley was committed to this
action. Doyle's raise was 88,000, so Bradley was required
to put at least 188,000 (the 12,000 blind, plus Doyle's
88,000 raise, plus 88,000 more) into the pot. Doyle had
TT and Bradley, who was merely trying to steal the blinds
and antes with A7, would almost certainly have folded had
Doyle's raise been clarified. When the cards were exposed,
Bradley was about a 2.5-1 underdog, but an ace flopped
and Doyle was eliminated. In this case, Bradley got very
lucky. But what if another player had a bigger hand and
re-raised Bradley? His innocent error could have knocked
him out of the biggest tournament in history!

An interesting aside: The source of the background
commotion was a round of applause from the crowd when
Blair was KO'd in 54th spot. He'd had a great World Series and tournament director Matt Savage gave him a nice
send-off. In a way, Blair knocked Doyle out of the Big
One!

The lesson of this story is that you must always be observant of everything going on around you and be very
careful about what you say.

Exposing Cards

In cash games, some players (especially some of the old-timers), when faced with a tough decision after all the cards have been dealt, like to expose their hole cards, hoping to get a reaction from their opponent. Puggy Pearson and Doyle are known for this. A few years back, a rule was passed against this practice. Doing so now can result in a penalty. Not only does this cover actually exposing your cards, but also verbally declaring your hand. The best advice for a beginning player is to keep quiet and don't show your cards until the showdown, after all betting is complete.

Dead Hand

If your hand is "dead," it's considered mucked. You can't continue on in that hand or collect any chips from the pot. Let's look at some examples of dead hands.

If you don't have exactly two cards in your hand, you've got a dead hand. If you bring it to the dealer's attention quickly, it'll probably be declared a misdeal. If you don't say anything before there's been significant action by the other players (usually two or more players having acted on their hands), your hand will be considered folded.

If your cards hit the muck, either by you tossing them in or the dealer scooping them in, your hand is usually dead. This rule has been relaxed somewhat in recent years. If it wasn't your fault and it's obvious which cards are yours, some tournament directors will allow the hand to be pulled out of the muck and kept in play. It's important for you to protect your cards. Put something on them, such as a chip or similar item. This, in theory, prevents your hand from being killed accidentally. However, we've seen instances where cards with a chip on them were swept in by the dealer and the hand was declared dead. As a further precaution, keep your cards close to you, out of the reach of the dealer or other players.

> **KEY POINT**: It's a player's responsibility to protect his hand at all times. Failure to do so may result in a hand being declared dead.

If you're away from the table when the cards are dealt, your hand is dead. There are two interpretations of this rule. At the WSOP and the Aussie Millions, if you're not in your seat when the last downcard is dealt, you've got a dead hand. At Bellagio, you have until it's your turn to act to return to your seat. We like the WSOP/Aussie Millions rule better. We don't like the scenario of a player returning to the table, walking behind us and possibly seeing our cards, then being allowed to play his hand.

If you have a card in your hand that's duplicated elsewhere, either in your hand or on the board, you must bring it to the attention of the dealer immediately. For instance, say you have two aces of spades in your hand or you have an ace of spades and another ace of spades hits the board. If you say nothing, figuring that if you win the hand without having to turn your hand up it's a freebie and if you don't win you can claim foul, your hand could, should, and probably will be declared dead. You'll forfeit any chips you had in the pot, even if you claim you didn't notice. Had you brought it to the dealer's attention before the hand played out, it would've likely been declared a misdeal and the cards would've been re-dealt.

Moving Tables

At multi-table tournaments, tables are condensed until there's only one left. At most tournaments, tables are "broken" as the need arises and players from the broken tables are assigned to the vacant seats at other tables. At most tournaments, when it's down to three tables, all players re-draw seats. When moving to a new table, you're supposed to go directly there without delay. Once there, you assume the rights and responsibilities of that seat. If it's your big blind, you must post it. If you get a free hand (you're dealt a hand in a non-blind position), it's yours to play. The only time you don't get a hand is if the seat you're taking is between the small blind and the button. In that case you must wait until the button passes your seat before you get dealt in.

Sometimes players try to delay sitting down at a new table if they see that they'd have to post the big blind right away. They try to stall until it passes. Avoiding the blinds, especially at later stages of a tournament, can be a big advantage to a player. This is unethical and against the rules, and could merit a penalty and forfeiture of the chips that would have gone in for the blind.

Another rule at most major tournaments is that chips must be kept in view at all times when moving tables. Chips may not be put in pockets, for example. The reason for this is that instances of cheating have occurred by players pocketing chips, either for use later in that tournament (to pass to other players) or to use in a later tournament at the same venue. These are grievous offenses that are dealt with harshly. Don't put chips in your pocket and risk being accused of these practices.

Soft Play

In tournament poker, every other player in the tournament should be your adversary. Everything that happens at every table has an effect on every player. Occasionally, two friends at the same table won't play their best against each other. In side games this is common and usually not significant. In tournaments, it's against the rules and can have a huge effect on the outcome.

For instance, once the field is whittled down to being in or close to the money, when a player is knocked out, it usually benefits the other players. If the tournament pays 18 places and 19 are left, it's important for players with short stacks to have another player eliminated (so they get a payday). If a player has a big hand against his friend and chooses to check on every betting round so as to not risk eliminating him, it's damaging to the other players, is unethical, and should be punished. Unfortunately, this is very hard to prove and remains a problem.

To take this a step further, say one friend has a big stack and his buddy is very short on chips. If he's involved in a pot with his buddy, he could put some chips in the pot by betting or calling, then fold, effectively transferring chips from his stack to his buddy's. This is a more serious offense than soft-playing, but again, is hard to prove. We think these are issues that need to be resolved as tournaments continue to grow and evolve.

Penalties

A few years back (originally at the WSOP, we believe), tournament directors began the practice of assessing penalties against players for various offenses. The original idea was to discourage misbehavior. In addition to the infractions discussed above, penalties can be assessed for foul language, abusing dealers or other players (either verbally or physically), throwing cards or chips off the table, intentionally bending or breaking cards or chips, and other such infractions. Penalties are usually assessed by requiring the offending player to spend a certain amount of time away from the table. While he's away, the player is missing hands, but is still posting blinds as if he were playing. The usual penalty for a first-time offender is 10 minutes, but more serious penalties can be assessed for repeated or more serious offenses. Very grievous infractions can result in disqualification from the tournament.

At the 2005 WSOP, a policy was instituted of penalizing players for use of the naughty f-word, or "f-bomb," as they referred to it. Players were unhappy with this policy. For one thing, it was selectively enforced. For another, this is poker, not a church function. Few players condone abuse of dealers or fellow players, but as long as the term isn't directed at someone, why the big deal?

The f-bomb rule at the 2005 WSOP led to some unusual situations. In one instance, a player reportedly slung the banned word heads-up at a final table! The floorman insisted on assessing the penalty. While the perpetrator sat in the penalty box, his opponent racked up undefended blinds. In another, with two tables left, the penalty was assessed, against a girl!

The most amusing incident, though, involved Mike "the mouth" Matusow at the start of the Big One. Mike was accused by the dealer of throwing the cards. When the floorman let him off with a warning (after the other players at the table supported his side), he let the word slip.

"Now I have to give you a ten-minute penalty," said the tournament director. "You can't say the f-word."

"Fuck that," Matusow shot back.

"Twenty minutes."

"Fuckin' great."

"Thirty minutes."

As Matusow was leaving the area, he managed to fire off one more f-bomb, rounding out his penalty to 40 minutes. The time out didn't hurt him too much, as he went on to finish ninth out of 5,619 players.

Miscellaneous

Some other things you should know:

Big Chips in Front—You're required to keep your biggest denomination chips in plain view. It's only fair that the other players can see your biggest chips to get an idea of how much you have. Some players may try to hide their big chips in an effort to misrepresent the size of their stack. If you do this, you'll usually be taken to task by the dealer or other players. Repeated attempts could result in a penalty. If a player's chips are hidden by his hands or in some other way, you have the right to ask to see them.

Speaking Up—Don't be afraid to say something when there's a controversy and you have information that could help solve the problem. For instance, if an ante is missing and you know which player didn't ante, say so. Often the player missed anteing by mistake. If a player put the incorrect amount in a pot or a dealer makes a mistake with the chips, speak up if you see it. Everything that happens in a tournament affects you, so it's generally in your best interest to see that things are done correctly. Another example is when a shown-down hand is misread, either by a player or the dealer. It's okay to point out the mistake. But be careful. A player's hand is only considered shown down on the end if it's turned face up on the table. Say a player has the winning hand, but is holding the cards off the table where only you and he can see them. You *don't* have the right, or obligation, to point out that he has the winner. In fact, doing so is considered unethical and is likely to get a heated reaction from other players.

Calling the Clock—If a player is taking a long time to act, any other player at the table has the right to call for a clock. This is a fairly rare occurrence. If it's a player who generally acts quickly, but is faced with a tough decision, the other players usually allow him plenty of leeway. A player who habitually takes a long time to act is more likely to have a clock called. Once the request is made, a floorman comes to the table and announces that the player has one minute to act. If the player doesn't act within this time, his hand is dead. While you have the right to call a clock at any time, be aware that some players take it very personally. An inexperienced player has enough to worry about and is probably better off avoiding this situation.

Side Pots—A side pot takes place when a player is all-in and active players are still in the pot. If you're the all-in player, it's improper to give any indication as to the strength of your hand, as doing so could influence the way the other players act on their hands. As far as the players still active, it's not unusual or unethical for them to check their hands to the end in order to have the best chance of eliminating the all-in player.

The matter of who shows his cards first at the end usually proceeds as follows.

• If there's no betting on the river, the first player to the left of the button is the first to expose his hand, and so on clockwise around the table. If a player can't beat an already-exposed hand, he's not required to show his hand.

• If there's betting on the river, the player who initiated the final action is first to expose. For example, if a player bets, gets raised, then calls the raise, the raiser opens his hand first. If more than two players are involved in the above situation, the player to the left of the player who initiated final action is the next to expose his hand, and so on around the table.

The above seems cut and dried but there are some complicating factors.

• If a player bluffs on the river and gets called, he'll sometimes say something like, "You got me," or he'll tap the table as an indication that his hand can't win. In most cases, the established etiquette is for the player who called to show his hand without requiring the bluffer to expose his. However, this isn't always the case. You have a right to see his hand, or you could tell him to muck his hand before you expose yours. Just remember, how you handle this is usually returned in kind when the situation is reversed.

• Any player at the table has the right to ask to see a losing hand. However, this is generally frowned on and will likely engender some animosity.

• In some cardrooms, the player who initiated last action is first to show, regardless of on which street the final action occurred. This occasionally causes a stir. However, in most cardrooms we've been in, the rule above applies.

ETHICS

Ploys of Questionable Ethics

We've stressed the importance of knowing the rules, which can vary from tournament to tournament. Some players are not averse to bending certain rules to their advantage, using what appears to be a mistake as a form of deception. It's important that you be both aware and wary of these potential ploys, so that you're not victimized or misled.

Using an Oversized Chip
Without Announcing "Raise"

As far as we know, all tournaments consider the betting of a single oversized chip, without an accompanying verbal declaration of the intention to raise, to be a call. We've discussed how this works in the section on rules. But sometimes this universal rule is abused.

Lets say that the blinds are 50-100 and it's passed to the button, who throws in a 500 chip, but says nothing. The dealer should announce, "That's a call." Now, the player who made the bet may act dismayed, indicating that his intention was to raise. He may do this either with his actions, or verbally by saying, "I meant to raise." Often this action is genuine, especially with players accustomed to online play. But occasionally it's a ploy. Think about it. In the above example, if the player using the oversized chip convinces the blinds that his true purpose was to raise, the small blind will likely get out of the way with most marginal hands. Why get involved out of position when the button's probably got a powerful holding?

As for the big blind, this ploy pretty well freezes him, unless he has a monster. What would you do with hands like pocket 8s through 10s or AJ suited, if you're convinced the button wanted to raise? Would you now risk raising, knowing that there's a good chance that your opponent will come back over the top for all your money? We certainly wouldn't. Better to see the flop cheaply and take it from there. The player on the button has frozen you with his ploy. If overcards now hit on the flop, as they will the majority of the time when you have a medium pair, what do you do? Since you suspect that your opponent has a strong hand, it's likely you'll check and fold when he bets, which he'll usually do. After all, you've got nothing at stake yet, except your blind. And you've missed the flop, which may very well have helped your opponent who has already indicated strength and is now betting. It looks like you've dodged a bullet and escaped for the absolute minimum.

What's actually come down, however, is a bit of subtle subterfuge. In reality, the button has a speculative hand and doesn't want to be raised. He may have suited connectors or a tiny pair, hands he wants to see a flop with cheaply. By feigning a desire to raise, he's accomplished multiple objectives.

• He's prevented a player who would normally have raised from doing so, enabling him to see a cheap flop.

• The small blind is likely to fold, limiting the field.

• He's indicated that he's strong when he's actually weak, allowing him to win many pots with a bet on the flop.

• And if he hits his hand, it will be well-disguised. If he has pocket 2s and the flop comes 7-5-2, his opponents can't possibly put him on a set and may get trapped with an over pair, such as 8s, 9s, or 10s.

As you can see, this player has reaped tremendous benefits at little cost. Some players are extremely talented at pulling off this move without saying a word—their actions, expressions, and body language clearly indicate their intention was to raise. If queried, they may even say, "No, I meant to call," which sounds like a lie, especially when everything else you observe screams out, "Of course I wanted to raise!" Their verbal protestations only serve to reinforce your erroneous conclusion and influence your play throughout the hand. This ploy is especially effective when the blinds and antes are high and there's more at stake.

We want to re-emphasize the fact that this bit of deception is not illegal. There's no possible penalty involved. The ethics can certainly be argued, but the legality is clear—an oversized chip without a verbal declaration is just a call.

We're not recommending that you use this ruse, but we believe it's important that you're aware of it, so you can act accordingly when it's encountered, especially when it's done by a known and experienced player.

Making an Under-Raise

Tournament rules differ as to what constitutes a raise when an insufficient amount of chips have been put into the pot. In some locations, it's anything half or more of the amount of the big blind pre-flop or the original bet post-flop; in other locations, even $5 short will not be considered a raise. Both variations are subject to manipulation.

Let's take an actual example from a recent tournament. With blinds of 300-600, it was passed around to the button who called the 600. The small blind folded and the big blind checked. The flop was 9-9-8 with two diamonds. The big blind checked and the button bet 700. Instead of calling with a 500 chip and two 100 chips, the player in the big blind threw in two 500 chips and one 100 chip, a total of 1,100. Mistake? Perhaps.

The player on the button asked, "Is that a raise?"

The raiser replied, "My intentions don't matter; get a ruling."

The tournament director was called and he explained that the rules call for any raise consisting of half the original bet or more be made up to the full amount of the bet, or the hand is dead and the chips remain in the pot. Dutifully, the raiser put in an additional 300, making his raise equal to the size of the original bet. Not knowing the raiser's real intention put the original bettor in a quandary. A mini-check-raise equal to the size of the bet is a very strong play, often indicating a big hand, but a check-call would be more commensurate with a drawing hand. Which was it?

The original bettor actually had A8, giving him 9s and 8s. If his opponent had a 9, he was practically drawing dead—even another 8 wouldn't help him. His opponent was an experienced tournament pro. After considerable deliberation, he decided to fold rather than call the 600 raise. He reasoned that it had to be a ploy, rather than a legitimate mistake, and was suspicious. Furthermore, if either a straight or flush card hit, neither of which would help him, the possibility that the raiser really did mean to call with a draw would now come into play. This combination of factors created enough doubt in his mind that he chose to be done with the hand then and there, rather than be subjected to a complex guessing game that could jeopardize a lot of his chips.

Whether the under-raise was a legitimate mistake or a ploy, we'll never know. The point is to know the rules, then evaluate your opponent as best you can. Having said this, it's often very difficult, even for pros, to judge the true intentions of deceptive players unless they've seen them make this same move before.

Stalling

Stalling is a relatively common tournament tactic for which there's currently no penalty, although most pros, including us, despise the tactic. It's most commonly seen when players are close to the money. At this juncture, some players with low stacks may deliberate about a decision for as much as several minutes, hoping that players at other tables will get knocked out in the interim, which puts them in the money. Such stalling reduces the number of hands played at the table, penalizing the players with solid stacks who have fewer opportunities to pick up additional chips.

One solution to the problem is to play "hand for hand."

This means that every table must complete the hand in progress before another hand is dealt at any table. In most tournaments, this is only done when it gets down to one player away from the money. At the final event of the 2005 WSOP, 560 places were paid. When there were 561 players left, the hand-for-hand policy was implemented—the largest hand for hand in live-tournament history.

If you suspect someone of stalling, you also have the option of calling for the clock, as previously discussed. Don't be shy about calling for the clock in situations where stalling negatively impacts your play.

Another time you may encounter stalling is when the blinds are about to go up and a player wants a favorable position at the new level. Say there's one minute left at a level before the blinds and antes go up and play is passed around to the button, who raises. The small blind, sitting on a low-to-medium stack, knows he's going to fold and suspects the big blind will also muck. He wants to have the button for the first hand at the new level, giving him a full round before he has to take the bigger blinds. So he acts as though he's thinking. Finally, when he knows there's not enough time left for the dealer to push the pot to the raiser, scramble, shuffle, and cut the cards prior to the new level being announced, he releases his hand. Given current tournament rules, there's no way to prevent this form of subtle manipulation.

While we don't condone stalling in any form, we do encourage you to be very aware of the time remaining at each level. Sometimes it pays to act on your hand instantly to move things along, aware that by expediting your play, the blinds are likely to pass you before the next level begins. No one will ever complain about, or resent, your acting on your hand too quickly.

Playing Out of Turn

Occasionally, a player acts out of turn. This can have a major effect on the way the hand plays out. Suppose the player first to act in a 3-player hand has a big hand and is trying to decide whether to bet or try for a check-raise, but the second player bets before he's acted. In most tournaments, if the first player now checks, the second player must bet an amount at least equal to the big blind. This is good for player 1, as he's now assured of the opportunity to raise. If only the two of them were involved in the hand, it wouldn't be so bad, as the player who made the mistake would be the one disadvantaged. In a 3-person game, however, the ramifications are more serious. The third player is in a bad spot. The possibility that the first player may now check-raise will probably make him more reluctant to get involved in the hand. He may miss a profitable opportunity.

The first player may also be adversely affected. If the third player folds when he would have called (had the second player not acted out of turn), it could be costly to player 1. You can see how the second player's error may significantly influence the way this hand plays out. The possibility of intentional abuse exists here.

Most of the time, acting out of turn is simply the result of a player not paying attention. Occasionally, however, a player will act out of turn to try to gain a strategic advantage. For instance, a player might check a big hand out of turn, hoping the player in front of him will see it as weakness and bet into him. We feel this is a major violation that should be dealt with harshly.

13

PHIL IS DEAD;
LONG LIVE PHIL

You get your chips your way and I'll get mine my way.
—Phil Ivey to Howard Lederer

The Worst-Kept Secret

No-limit hold 'em is a wonderfully intricate game when played in a ring for cash. However, it doesn't translate ideally into a tournament game. The Kill Phil strategy is designed to take advantage of what we, and many others, feel is a weakness in no-limit hold 'em tournaments—the overemphasis on the all-in move in the later stages.

In the period leading up to the publication of this book, it was clear that the "secret" was out. More and more players were employing move-in tactics of various kinds, especially in the latter stages of NLH tournaments, when it matters most. Kill Phil will exacerbate this situation. Is this good for poker?

To take things to the extreme, let's assume that this book proves immensely popular and half the players in the next WSOP are wearing Kill Phil hats and carrying Kill Phil strategy cards. If the poker-viewing public is as entranced by the showdown scenario as they appear to be, Kill Phil will do nothing but give them more of what they want and, potentially in the process, bring a whole new wave of players to the game.

On the other hand, television producers we've spoken with believe that if poker's long-term future is to be guaranteed, it needs to become a sport. Beginners can't compete on even footing with today's NFL and NBA stars, so why should they be allowed to do so in poker tournaments, due to a flaw in the no-limit structure? What if poker viewers mature and indicate through their viewing habits that they're ready to move past the scenario of one showdown after another? Will Kill Phil have hurt poker?

No! For starters, fixing the flaw that makes the Kill Phil strategy effective isn't that difficult. Eliminating the all-in option pre-flop would be a simple step. A combination of pot-limit in the earlier betting rounds with no-limit in the later rounds would render the Kill Phil strategy pretty much useless. That format would mandate more flops, adding complexity and excitement for both players and audiences alike. We're sure that the better players would readily agree. Daniel Negreanu made his opinion perfectly clear in an article in the May 10, 2002, issue of *Card Player*. In it he referenced Sklansky's *System* and expressed his consternation at the direction no-limit tournaments were headed. Referring to moving all-in before the flop, he said, "The most annoying part about this is that once the blinds and antes have reached a certain level, what they're doing can actually become a winning strategy." His opinion, that pot-limit is a more accurate test of skill, is echoed by many good players.

The Future of Tournament Play

To take it a step further, at the Aussie Millions in Melbourne in 2005, a new style of poker was spotlighted in a special televised event (won by Lee Nelson) that combined a structure of pot-limit pre-flop and no-limit post-flop with another innovation called "Speed Poker," in which players had only 15 seconds to act on their hands. We feel that, with a little tweaking, the Speed Poker aspect would solve the growing problem of players taking too long to act, as well as make it much more exciting for spectators. This approach is good for the players, the casinos, and poker fans. It solves some of the logistical problems presented by the huge and ever-growing fields. It allows television producers to stage live poker events, which fits perfectly into the goal of making it a sport. Getting around twice as many hands per hour accommodates slower escalating structures, giving better players time to work their magic, while also making it deadly for Phil Killers. We predict that some version of this format will eventually become the standard for televised poker.

The publication of this book isn't an attempt on our part to hurt the game. We love poker. Eventually, either through someone else publishing some version of the strategy we've presented here or simply through the growing realization that the all-in move is so effective for the inexperienced player, poker would reach the aforementioned crossroads. We're merely pointing out the elephant standing in the corner. If our work helps to propel poker to the next level, whatever that may be, we'll be happy.

The effectiveness of the KP strategy in no-limit tournaments as they're presently structured opens the door for new players to play, observe, and learn the game, while having a realistic chance of success along the way. Take advantage of this. Move beyond the KP Basic as quickly as possible. Once you've gotten everything you can out of our book, read and study other good books on the other facets of the game.

Implementation of the structural changes discussed above would make it much more difficult for new players to get the real-time experience necessary to improve their skills. For aspiring players, now is the time to enter the arena. This window of opportunity may not be open much longer.

APPENDIX I

POKER HANDS
(in ascending value)

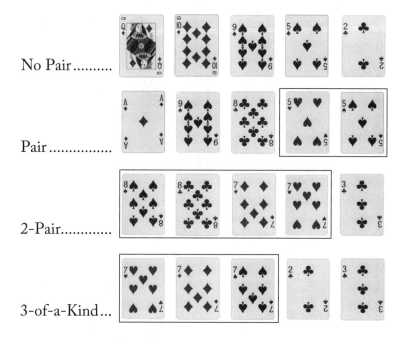

No Pair..........

Pair...............

2-Pair.............

3-of-a-Kind...

Straight..........

Flush.............

Full House.....

4-of-a-Kind...

Straight Flush

Royal Flush....

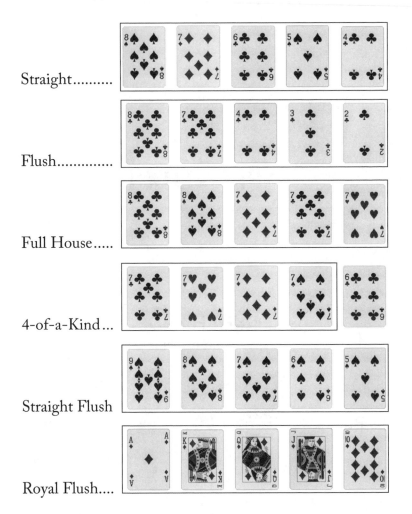

APPENDIX II

BASICS OF NO-LIMIT TEXAS HOLD 'EM

A game of Texas hold 'em, or simply hold 'em as it's known, begins with each player being dealt two cards face down. In casinos and public cardrooms, a house dealer shuffles and deals the cards, beginning with the player to the left of the "button," which represents the designated dealer position for that hand. The button moves clockwise around the table, one player at a time, after the completion of each hand.

The player to the immediate left of the button is known as the "small blind." To his left is the "big blind." These players must post mandatory bets, designed to initiate the betting action. The amount of the small blind is generally half that of the big blind. Action starts with the player to the left of the big blind. His options are to "fold" (toss or push his cards face down to the dealer, being careful not to expose them), "call" the amount of the big blind, or "raise" an amount at least equal to the amount of the blind. For example, if the blinds are 100-200, a player can fold, call 200, or raise to at least 400. In no-limit, a player can raise anywhere from the minimum up to all the chips he has in front of him. Play continues in turn clockwise around the table in this manner.

If a player has raised, the next player can fold, call the raise, or re-raise an amount at least equal to the previous raise. To continue the above example, if the previous player has raised to 800, the next player may fold, call 800, or raise to at least 1,400 (the 800 represented a raise of 600 more than the 200 blind, so the re-raise must include that amount, plus at least 600 more). This continues until all players have had a chance to act, including the blinds, and any player whose action has been raised by another player.

On occasions where the action comes back around to the blinds without a raise, the small blind has the option to fold, call the big blind (essentially, making half a bet), or raise. If the small blind doesn't raise, the big blind has the option to raise, but he may also simply "check" (same as a call). This concludes the pre-flop action.

The dealer then turns three cards face up in the middle of the table. This is known as the "flop." These are community cards, that can be used by all players to form their hands. The action starts with the first involved player to the left of the button. He can check (not bet, with the option to call or raise any subsequent action) by saying "check" or by making an obvious tapping motion on the table. (Be careful not to make any motions that could be construed as a check if that's not your intention.) Or he can bet any amount from the size of the big blind up to all the chips he has in front of him. Action continues around the table in this manner. If there has been action in front of him, a player may fold, call the amount of the last action, or raise up to his entire stack.

When the action on the flop is completed, the dealer turns another single card face up next to the flop cards. This is known as the "turn," or "fourth street," and can also be used by all players to form their hands. Action on the turn works the same as on the flop.

Finally, the dealer turns up the "river" card, or "fifth street," after which the final round of betting takes place. When the betting is concluded, the players turn over their cards to determine the winner. The best five-card poker hand is culled from each player's two hole cards and the five community cards. If one or more players tie with the same-value hand, the pot is split accordingly.

All-In Pots

Any time only a single player in a contested pot will have chips remaining if he loses, it's an "all-in" pot and the players turn over their cards (regardless of the point they are at in the hand). The dealer deals the remaining cards and the winner is determined.

Side Pots

If one player is all-in, but there are still two or more players with chips, a "side pot" is created. The player who's all-in is eligible to win only an amount corresponding to the amount of chips he contributed to the main pot. If the other players continue to bet, they contest the side pot among themselves. If betting action is still possible, be careful not to expose your hand until the betting rounds are completed or until there's only one player still with chips.

Two Other Points

One of the dealer's functions is to keep the bets straight. Place your bets in front of you, rather than tossing the chips into the pot (known as "splashing the pot"), and let the dealer make change, if necessary.

Protect your cards when involved in a hand by placing something, such as a chip, on top of them. Unprotected hands run the risk of being scooped in by the dealer or being declared a "dead hand" if other cards should inadvertently become mingled with them.

APPENDIX III

HOW NO-LIMIT HOLD 'EM TOURNAMENTS WORK

A tournament begins with players posting a buy-in, the total of which generally makes up the prize pool. In addition to the buy-in, most tournaments charge an entry fee, which goes directly to the house. For instance, a tournament listed as $1,000+$60, with 100 players entering, would have a prize pool of $100,000 and a house fee of $6,000. Some tournaments, such as the WSOP, don't list the entry fee separately, but this doesn't mean the house doesn't take its cut. Out of the $100,000 collected, the house takes a percentage, say 6%, then distributes the remainder as prize money. In addition, it's become the norm for most big tournaments to withhold an additional 3% of the prize fund as gratuities for the tournament's dealers and staff.

In the above tournament, the field would be divided

by a random draw into 10 tables of 10 players each. Each player is given the same amount of chips to begin the tournament. Once a player loses all his chips, he's eliminated from the tournament (unless it's a "re-buy" tournament, in which case players have the option to buy more chips for a certain period of time). As players are eliminated, the tables are condensed until there's only one table remaining, known as the final table. Play continues until one player has all the chips.

In order to ensure that the tournament ends within a reasonable period of time, the blinds are increased according to a pre-determined schedule at set intervals. At some point in most no-limit tournaments, players are required to post antes in addition to the blinds.

The prize money is divided on a graduated basis among the highest finishers. The current trend is to pay up to 10% of the field. First place usually gets in the neighborhood of 35% of the prize pool. The lowest positions on the prize ladder generally get the amount of their buy-in, plus a small profit.

APPENDIX IV

GLOSSARY

3-of-a-kind—When a pair contained in the community cards matches one in your hand.

Aces cracked—When aces get beat, they're said to "get cracked."

All-in—Bet all your chips.

Ante—An amount put into the pot by each player prior to the deal.

Around back—The last 3 positions to act before the blinds.

Ax—An ace and a small card.

Baby—A small card.

Bad beat—Losing with a heavily favored hand.

Big ace—A starting hold 'em hand consisting of an ace with a big kicker.

Big hand—A very powerful hand.

Big slick—A starting hold 'em hand of AK.

Blind—A mandatory bet put up by the two players to the left of the button to start the action. The **small blind** is immediately to the left of the button. It's generally half the size of the **big blind,** which is two seats to the left of the button and acts last before the flop.

Bluff—Betting or raising with a very weak hand.

Bluff-call—Calling on a betting round with a poor hand, with the intention of bluffing on later rounds.

Board—The community cards in a hold 'em hand.

Bubble (skunk-hole in Australia)—One position away from the prize money.

Bust out—Lose all your chips.

Button—The player with dealer position who's last to act prior to the blinds pre-flop and last to act on each round post-flop.

Buy-in—The amount of money required to be put up by each player to participate in a tournament.

Call for the clock—Requesting the tournament director to give a player one minute to act on his hand.

Call—Match an opponent's bet.

Calling station—A player who rarely bets or raises and calls too frequently.

Case card—The last card of a particular rank left in the deck. For example, if there are three 8s on the board, the last 8 is referred to as the case 8.

Cash game—A poker game for real money, as opposed to a tournament, which is contested for tournament chips that have no cash value. Also known as a side game.

Check—To not bet. A player indicates this by saying "check" or tapping on the table.

Check it down—At times, especially as an inexperienced player, you'll be happy not to have to make any more decisions on a hand. If you check on the remaining betting rounds and your opponent checks along with you, then the best hand will win.

Check-raising—Checking, with the intention of raising, if your opponent bets.

Coin flip—A confrontation between two hands that's close to an even-money proposition, such as a pair versus two overcards.

Cold call—Calling a bet and a raise.

Come over the top—Re-raise.

Concealed hand—A hand in which both cards are used to make a hand.

Connected flop—A flop that lends itself to a flush, or straight draws, or both. For instance, a flop of 6♣-8♣-9♦ could give a variety of hands a draw at a big hand. Any hand with two clubs, or holdings such as 7-6, 8-7, 9-7, T-9, T-8, J-T would give a player a draw to a straight, or flush.

Counting outs—Determining the number of cards that would turn a losing hand into a winning one, either on the turn or the river.

CPR—Abbreviation for cost-per-round.

Crying call—A call that's justified due to the size of the pot, but doesn't figure to win.

CSI—Abbreviation for chip-status index.

Cut-off—The position immediately to the right of the button.

Dead money—A player with little chance of winning.

Define your hand—Make a bet that helps to determine the relative strength of your hand by gauging your opponents' reactions.

Desperado—A player with a very short stack.

Dominated—A match-up of two pre-flop hold 'em hands, where the top card is identical and the kicker (side-card) is of lower rank in the dominated hand. AQ is said to be dominated by AK.

Draw out—When a hand that's an underdog catches cards to make it a winning hand.

Drawing dead—A hand with no chance of winning regardless of what additional cards come.

Drawing live—A situation where there are cards left in the deck that will make a hand that's behind into a winner also known as drawing dead.

Dry pot—A side pot into which there can be no more betting.

Entry fee—An amount posted by each player in addition to the buy-in. The entry fee generally goes directly to the hosting establishment. For example, in a tournament will be listed as $1,500+$70, the $1,500 goes into the prize pool and the $70 goes to the house.

Event—A specific contest within a tournament schedule at a certain location. For instance, the 2005 WSOP consists of more than 40 separate events.

Favorite—A hand having more than a 50% chance of winning.

Feeler bet—A bet made with the intention of gauging an opponent's hand by his reaction.

Find out where you're at—*See* Define your hand.

Fire a second barrel—A bluff on the turn, after having bluffed on the flop.

Fire a third barrel—A bluff on the river, after having bluffed on the flop and the turn.

Flop—Three community cards exposed simultaneously, after which there's a round of betting.

Fold—Discard your hand.

Free card—Seeing the next card without having to put in any chips.

Garbage—A poor hand.

Get played with—When an opponent decides to call a bet or raise.

Get a line on your play—When an opponent forms an impression about the way you play.

Go into the tank—Think for a long time before acting on a hand.

Have a player covered—When you have more chips than an opponent.

Heads-up—Only two contestants.

Hole cards—The two cards dealt facedown to each player at the beginning of a hand.

Jump the fence—When it appears as though two players are involved in a hand and a third player becomes involved by calling a raise or re-raise.

Kicker—A side card that often decides the outcome of a hand when both players have the same pair.

Lay down—Fold.

Limit—A blind, or blind and ante, level. This usage is common among players, even though they're referring to no-limit poker.

Limiting the field—Reducing the number of opponents, usually by raising.

Limper—A player who enters a pot by calling the amount of the big blind.

Look up—Calling a bet at the end of a hand, forcing an opponent to show his cards.

Main pot—A pot eligible to be won by any player who has contributed an amount equal to that of the other involved players. If two players have bet a greater number of chips than a third player, it goes into a separate pot, called a side-pot. The side-pot can be won only by contributing players.

Make a move—When a player makes a substantial bet or raise (often all-in) that's either a bluff or semi-bluff.

Maniac—A wild unpredictable player.

Mini-raise—A smaller-than-average raise, usually the minimum or slightly higher.

Mix up your play—To play unpredictably.

Monster—A big hand.

Move in—*See* All-in.

Move-in specialist or MIS—A player who uses the all-in move as a primary tactic.

Muck—Same as fold.

Multi-way pot—A pot contested by more than two players.

Newbie—A player new to poker.

Nuts—A cinch hand.

Nut flush—The best possible flush.

Nut straight—The best possible straight.

Out—A card that would convert a hand from a loser to a winner.

Overbet a pot—To make a bet larger than the size of the pot.

Overcards—Cards in your hand that are bigger than those on the board.

Over-pair—A pocket pair higher in rank than any of the exposed community cards on the board.

Overlay—Getting better odds than you should get, based on expectation.

Overplay—Play a hand too strongly.

Pace of play—Aggression or lack of aggression at a table as a whole.

Pick up the pot (or the blinds)—Win the blinds, or a small pot, with a relatively weak hand.

Piece of cheese—A bad hand. Also sometimes referred to as trash or garbage.

Play back at—Re-raise.

Play the board—When your best hand consists of the five community cards.

Pocket pair—Two down cards of the same rank.

Pocket rockets—A starting hand of two aces.

Position—A player's turn in the betting rotation.

Positive equity—A situation that's mathematically favorable.

Pot-committed—Having such a high percentage of a stack already in the pot that a fold is unlikely.

Pot-odds—The amount of money in the pot relative to the cost of calling. For example, if there's $1,000 in the pot and it costs you $500 to call your opponent's bet or raise, you're getting pot-odds of 1,000-500, or 2-1.

Pot-size manipulation—Using the size of bets to manipulate the odds the pot is offering an opponent.

Probing bet—A bet made with the intention of gaining information about the strength of an opponent's hand.

Put a player on a hand—Making a judgment as to an opponent's holding.

Put to a decision—Make a significant bet at an opponent.

Quads—4-of-a-kind.

Quality hand—A good hand.

Race-Showdown with more cards to come; often used to describe a showdown between a pair and two overcards.

Rainbow flop—A flop containing three cards of different suits.

Raise—Match an opponent's bet and bet an additional amount.

Read (a player)—Use clues to estimate an opponent's hand.

Reasonable bet—A bet of a normal size for a given situation.

Re-steal—Bluff a bluffer.

Reverse tell—An intentional ploy of using mannerisms to mislead an opponent.

Ring game—*See* Cash game.

River, or fifth street—A final single community card exposed after betting has concluded on the turn card, after which there's a final round of betting.

Rush—A player winning a series of pots is said to be "on a rush."

Scare card—A turn or river card that causes a player to fear that his opponent has completed a hand.

Second pair—A hole card that matches the second highest card on the board.

Semi-bluff—Betting, or raising, with a hand that's currently weak, but could develop into a strong hand. Examples are straight, or flush, draws.

Set—3-of-a-kind using both cards from your hand and one from the board.

Short-handed play—Playing with less than a full table of players.

Showdown—Exposing your cards when all the cards are dealt and determining the winner of the hand.

Side-game—*See* Cash game.

Side-pot—A pot that contains chips not eligible to be won by an active player who hasn't contributed to it.

Slow-play—Playing a strong hand weakly in the hopes of misleading an opponent as to the strength of your hand, thereby trapping him for some, or all, of his chips at a later point in the hand. Examples of slow-playing would be checking when your hand is obviously strong enough to bet or smooth-calling a bet by an opponent whose hand you're pretty sure is weaker than yours.

Small blind-big blind confrontation—A pot in which everyone has folded around to the small blind.

Smooth- or flat-call—To call a bet with a hand that's strong enough to raise with.

Snapping off a bluff—Calling a bet, or raise, when an opponent is bluffing.

Sponsor—A backer who puts up entry fees, and often expense money, for a player. Any profits are split on an agreed-upon percentage. This can be either an individual or a corporation.

Slow-rolling—Hesitating before turning over a winning hand. Considered bad form by many players.

Speculative hand—A relatively weak hand that can develop into a big hand.

Stand much heat—A hand that must fold to a significant bet, as in "his hand couldn't stand much heat."

Standard-sized bet (or raise)—A normal bet (or raise) for that particular situation.

Steal the blinds—*See* Pick up the pot.

Steal positions—The positions where players are more likely to try to steal the blinds and antes: one before the button (cut-off), the button, and the small blind.

Structure—The schedule according to which the blinds and antes increase throughout the tournament.

Suited connectors—A starting hold 'em hand with two cards of the same suit in sequence (example: 4-5 of spades).

Tell—A mannerism that gives a clue as to the value of a player's hand. A player spotting such a mannerism in an opponent is said to "pick up a tell."

Texture of a flop—Relationship of the three flop cards to each other.

Third pair—A hole card that matches the third highest pair on the board.

Tilt—Playing uncharacteristically recklessly, usually as a result of one or more bad beats.

Tolerance for ambiguity—Able to handle uncertainty.

Top pair—A card in your hand of the same rank as the highest exposed community card.

Tournament—An entire schedule of individual events at a given location. Sometimes the individual events are also referred to as tournaments.

Turn, or fourth street—A single community card exposed after betting is completed on the flop, after which there's another round of betting.

Two-card hold 'em—A manner of play where most of the betting is done pre-flop, such as by Kill Phil players.

Unconnected flop—A flop that doesn't lend itself to straight or flush draws, such as K♦-8♣-3♠.

Underdog (or dog)—A hand having less than a 50% chance of winning.

Under the gun—The player immediately to the left of the big blind, who must act first before the flop.

Up-front—The first three positions to act.

Value bet—A bet made with what is likely to be the best hand at the time, but is not the best possible hand.

Wake up with a hand—Pick up a very strong starting hand.

Weak ace—A starting hold 'em hand consisting of an ace with a small kicker.

Weak-tight—A player who plays only strong hands and plays them timidly.

World's Fair—A powerful hand.

WPT—World Poker Tour.

WSOP—World Series of Poker.

Zero-sum game—A game in which wins and losses offset.

APPENDIX V

PRE-FLOP MATCH-UPS
(based on EV)

A♣ K♦
vs.   AK is a 7-5 favorite
4♠ 5♠

A♣ K♦
vs.   AK is a 8-5 favorite
2♠ 3♠

A♠ K♦
vs.   AK almost 3-1 favorite
A♣ Q♥

A♣ K♦
vs.   22 is a 11-10 favorite
2♠ 2♣

A♣ K♦
vs.
T♠ T♥
(or JJ, QQ)

pairs are slightly more than
13-10 favorites

A♣ K♦
vs.
5♠ 5♦

55 is more than a 6-5 favorite

A♣ K♦
vs.
8♥ 8♠ (or 9-9)

pairs are 12½-10 favorites

A♠ K♠
vs.
2♥ 2♦

Even

J♠ T♠
vs.
4♦ 2♦

JT is a 9-5 favorite

A♠ K♥
vs.
4♦ 2♦

AK is more than an 8-5 favorite

A♣ K♥
vs.
J♦ T♦

AK is a 7-5 favorite

A♠ K♠
vs.
7♦ 8♣

AKs is a 9-5 favorite

A♠ A♦
vs.
K♥ K♣

AA is nearly a 4½-1 favorite

APPENDIX VI

POST-FLOP MATCH-UPS
(based on EV)

HANDS	FLOP	FAVORITE
8♥ 9♥ J♠ Q♠	3♥ 4♥ J♣	JQ is an 8-5 favorite
A♥ K♥ J♠ Q♠	3♥ 4♥ J♣	AK is a 6-5 favorite
Q♥ K♥ J♠ Q♠	3♥ 4♥ J♣	QK is a 11-10 favorite
T♥ J♥ Q♣ Q♠	3♥ 4♥ J♣	Even

5♥ 6♥
A♣ A♠   3♥ 4♥ J♠   56 is a 13-10 favorite

6♥ 6♦
A♣ A♠   3♥ 4♥ 5♣   AA is a7-5 favorite

K♣ Q♣
A♥ T♠   T♣ 9♣ 2♦   KQ is an 8-5 favorite

K♣ Q♣
A♥ T♠   T♣ 4♣ 2♦   KQ is a 6-5 favorite

K♣ Q♣
A♥ J♠   J♣ T♦ 2♦   Even

A♠ Q♦
8♥ 4♥   5♣ 8♦ 9♦   84 is a 2½-1 favorite

APPENDIX VII

PROBABILITY OF WINNING A SHOWDOWN WITH
A♦K♥ VS. BLACK PAIRS
(tie hands excluded)

BLACK PAIR WINS		A♦ K♥ WINS
QQ	56.99%	42.66%
JJ	57.09%	42.58%
TT	57.12%	42.57%

TT, JJ, and QQ all are more than 13/10 favorites over the AK.

99	55.53%	44.16%
88	55.42%	44.28%
77	55.25%	44.47%
66	55.23%	44.46%

BLACK PAIR WINS		A♦ K♥ WINS
55	54.82%	44.79%
44	54.21%	45.35%
33	53.52%	45.98%
22	52.75%	46.67%

All these pairs are about 12.5-10 favorites over AK.

APPENDIX VIII

OUTS

Odds of Making Your Hand with 2 Cards to Come

NUMBER OF OUTS	ODDS
20	2-1 favorite
18	8-5 favorite
15	6-5 favorite
14	51% favorite
13	48% underdog
12	6-5 underdog

Odds Against Making Your Hand with 1 Card to Come Depending On the Number of Outs

Assuming 44 cards left (accounting for your two cards, the 4 cards on the board, and your opponent's two cards):

8 outs—4.5-1 against

9 outs—about 4-1 against

10 outs—3.4-1 against

11 outs—3-1 against

12 outs—2.7-1 against

13 outs—2.4-1 against

14 outs—2.1-1 against

15 outs—slightly less than 2-1

18 outs—1.4-1 against

21 outs—11-10 against

Outs and Types of Hands that Provide Them

8 outs—open-ended straight draw

9 outs—flush draw with no overcards

10 outs—open-ended straight draw + pair

11 outs—open-ended straight draw with 1 overcard; flush draw + pair

12 outs—flush draw with 1 overcard

13 outs—flush draw + gutshot straight draw

14 outs—straight draw with 2 overcards

15 outs—flush draw with 2 overcards; flush draw + open-ended straight draw and no overcards

18 outs—flush draw with 2 overcards + gutshot straight draw; flush draw + open-ended straight draw + 1 overcard

21 outs—flush draw + straight draw + 2 overcards

APPENDIX IX

PAIR PROBABILITY
(AA through 22)

Your Hand	AA	KK	QQ	JJ	TT	99	88	77	66
Players to Act									
1	.995	.990	.986	.981	.977	.972	.968	.963	.959
2	.991	.981	.973	.964	.955	.946	.937	.928	.920
3	.986	.973	.959	.946	.933	.920	.907	.895	.882
4	.982	.964	.946	.929	.912	.895	.879	.862	.846
5	.978	.955	.933	.912	.891	.871	.851	.831	.812
6	.973	.946	.921	.896	.871	.847	.824	.801	.779
7	.969	.938	.908	.879	.851	.824	.798	.772	.747
8	.964	.929	.896	.864	.832	.802	.772	.744	.717
9	.960	.921	.884	.848	.813	.780	.748	.717	.687

Your Hand	55	44	33	22
Players to Act				
1	.954	.950	.945	.941
2	.911	.902	.894	.885
3	.870	.857	.845	.833
4	.830	.815	.799	.784
5	.793	.774	.756	.738
6	.757	.736	.715	.695
7	.723	.699	.676	.654
8	.690	.664	.639	.615
9	.659	.631	.605	.579

The chart shows the probability that "n" players yet to act will *not* have a pair of equal or greater rank when you begin with a pair of your own. The probability that you'll be dealt a pair 22-AA is approximately .059.

APPENDIX X

DEAL FORMULA
(Probability of player "A" finishing 1st, 2nd,
or 3rd depending on chip position)

CHIP PERCENTAGES			PROBABILITY		
A	B	C	A 1st	A 2nd	A Last
10%	10%	80%	0.100	0.405	0.495
10%	20%	70%	0.100	0.233	0.667
10%	30%	60%	0.100	0.160	0.740
10%	40%	50%	0.100	0.132	0.768
20%	10%	70%	0.200	0.495	0.305
20%	20%	60%	0.200	0.336	0.464
20%	30%	50%	0.200	0.261	0.539
20%	40%	40%	0.200	0.238	0.562
30%	10%	60%	0.300	0.494	0.206
30%	20%	50%	0.300	0.376	0.324
30%	30%	40%	0.300	0.322	0.378
40%	10%	50%	0.400	0.460	0.140
40%	20%	40%	0.400	0.381	0.219

CHIP PERCENTAGES			PROBABILITY		
A	B	C	A 1st	A 2nd	A Last
40%	30%	30%	0.400	0.355	0.245
50%	10%	40%	0.500	0.408	0.092
50%	20%	30%	0.500	0.363	0.137
60%	10%	30%	0.600	0.345	0.055
60%	20%	20%	0.600	0.327	0.073
70%	10%	20%	0.700	0.273	0.027
80%	10%	10%	0.800	0.191	0.009

Note: The probability of finishing first is always proportional to stack size, but the probability of finishing second is non-linear. Note the difference in second-place equity between a 10%-20%-70% chip distribution and a 20%-10%-70% distribution. Doubling the chips doubles first-place equity and more than doubles second-place equity.

APPENDIX XI

RECOMMENDED READING AND WEB SITES

Books

Brunson, Doyle. *Super/System*, 3rd ed. New York, NY: Cardoza Publishing, 2002.

Brunson, Doyle. *Super System 2*. New York, NY: Cardoza Publishing, 2005.

Cloutier, T.J., and Tom McEvoy. *Championship No-Limit & Pot-Limit Hold 'Em*. New York, NY: Cardoza Publishing, 2004.

Harrington, Dan, and Bill Robertie. *Harrington on Hold 'Em*. Vol. 1, *Strategic Play*. Henderson, NV: Two Plus Two Publishing, 2004.

Harrington, Dan, and Bill Robertie. *Harrington on Hold 'Em.* Vol. 2, *The Endgame.* Henderson, NV: Two Plus Two Publishing, 2005.

Reuben, Stewart, and Bob Ciaffone. *Pot-Limit and No-Limit Poker,* 2nd ed. Self-published, 1999.

Sklansky, David. *The Theory of Poker,* 4th ed. Henderson, NV: Two Plus Two Publishing, 1999.

Sklansky, David. *Tournament Poker for Advanced Players,* 2nd ed. Henderson, NV: Two Plus Two Publishing, 2003.

Smith, Dana; Tom McEvoy; and Ralph Wheeler. *The Championship Table.* New York, NY: Cardoza Publishing, 2004.

RECOMMENDED WEB SITES

Poker Players' Web Sites
Kill Phil (Blair and Lee):
killphilpoker.com
Daniel Negreanu's Web site:
fullcontactpoker.com
Paul Phillips' Journal Web site:
extempore.livejournal.com
Barry Greenstein's Web site:
barrygreenstein.com
Howard Lederer's Web site:
howardlederer.com
Phil Hellmuth's Web site:
philhellmuth.com

General-Information Web Sites
Card Player Web site:
cardplayer.com
Poker in Australia/New Zealand Web site:
pokernetwork.com
Two Plus Two Web site:
twoplustwo.com

Poker Tournament Information
U.S.—pokerpages.com
Europe—pokereuropa.net
Australia/New Zealand—pokernetwork.com

INDEX

About the Authors

Blair Rodman made it into the prize money six times and played at three final tables in the 2004 WSOP. He topped it off finishing 54th out of 2,576 players (one spot behind the legendary Doyle Brunson). Blair continued the pace in 2005, making two final tables on the  WSOP circuit, finishing second in the World Poker Tour finale at the Reno Hilton for a $327,000 payday, as well as second place at the Ultimate Poker Challenge at the Union Plaza.

 Lee Nelson has been the top-rated tournament player in Australia/New Zealand since 2000. In January 2006, he won the main event at the Aussie Millions and its approximatley $1,000,000us first prize. Lee also won the 2005 Party Poker World Open and its $400,000 prize. Making final tables with remarkable regularity in international tournaments, Lee's been dubbed with the nickname "Final Table."

KILL PHIL
STRATEGY CARDS

Now you can bring a condensed version of the Kill Phil strategies with you to live tournaments with our handy strategy cards: Kill Phil Rookie, Basic Live (including final-table/sit-n-go strategy), and Advanced Strategy Post-Flop Play. There's also a Basic Online card, for use as a quick reference when playing at home. Buy the set for $14.95

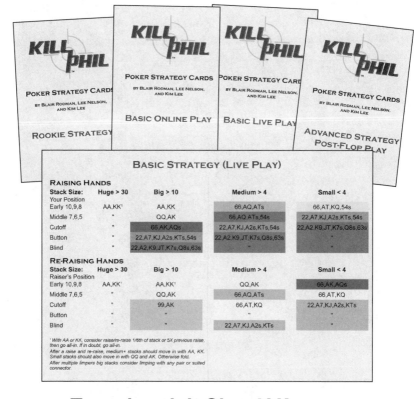

BASIC STRATEGY (LIVE PLAY)

RAISING HANDS

Stack Size: Your Position	Huge > 30	Big > 10	Medium > 4	Small < 4
Early 10,9,8	AA,KK¹	AA,KK	66,AQ,ATs	66,AT,KQ,54s
Middle 7,6,5	"	QQ,AK	66,AQ,ATs,54s	22,A7,KJ,A2s,KTs,54s
Cutoff	"	66,AK,AQs	22,A7,KJ,A2s,KTs,54s	22,A2,K9,JT,K7s,Q8s,63s
Button	"	22,A7,KJ,A2s,KTs,54s	22,A2,K9,JT,K7s,Q8s,63s	"
Blind	"	22,A2,K9,JT,K7s,Q8s,63s	"	"

RE-RAISING HANDS

Stack Size: Raiser's Position	Huge > 30	Big > 10	Medium > 4	Small < 4
Early 10,9,8	AA,KK¹	AA,KK¹	QQ,AK	66,AK,AQs
Middle 7,6,5	"	QQ,AK	66,AQ,ATs	66,AT,KQ
Cutoff	"	99,AK	66,AT,KQ	22,A7,KJ,A2s,KTs
Button	"	"	"	"
Blind	"	"	22,A7,KJ,A2s,KTs	"

¹ With AA or KK, consider raise/re-raise 1/6th of stack or 5X previous raise, then go all-in. If in doubt, go all-in.
After a raise and re-raise, medium+ stacks should move in with AA, KK. Small stacks should also move in with QQ and AK. Otherwise fold.
After multiple limpers big stacks consider limping with any pair or suited connector.

To order visit ShopLVA.com

ShopLVA.com
For Other Great
Poker Books and Products

Go to ShopLVA.com to find the best gambling books, software, DVDs, and strategy cards for all the casino games. All products at ShopLVA.com are endorsed by Anthony Curtis and the Las Vegas Advisor for their mathematical accuracy. ShopLVA.com is your source for the world's best gambling-strategy products.

Call 800-244-2224 for the Shop LVA catalog.
Or go to ShopLVA.com for the online catalog.

Visit
LasVegasAdvisor.com
for all the latest on gambling and Las Vegas

Free features include:

- Articles and ongoing updates on gambling.

- Tournament listings and articles

- Up-to-the-minute Las Vegas gambling promotion announcements.

- Question of the Day Offering in-depth answers to gambling and Las Vegas related queries.

- Active message boards with discussions on blackjack, sports betting, poker, and more!

Or become a *Las Vegas Advisor* Member and get our exclusive coupons and members-only discounts.

ABOUT HUNTINGTON PRESS

Huntington Press is a specialty publisher of Las Vegas- and gambling-related books and periodicals, including the award-winning consumer newsletter, *Anthony Curtis' Las Vegas Advisor.* To receive a copy of the Huntington Press catalog, call **1-800-244-2224** or write to the address below.

Huntington Press
3665 South Procyon Avenue
Las Vegas, Nevada 89103